PEARY'S ARCTIC QUEST

UNTOLD STORIES FROM ROBERT E. PEARY'S NORTH POLE EXPEDITIONS

SUSAN A. KAPLAN *and* GENEVIEVE M. LeMOINE

Down East Books

Camden, Maine

Down East Books

An imprint of Globe Pequot, the trade division of
The Rowman & Littlefield Publishing Group, Inc.
4501 Forbes Blvd., Ste. 200
Lanham, MD 20706
www.rowman.com

Published in cooperation with The Peary-MacMillan Arctic Museum, Bowdoin College, Brunswick, Maine

Distributed by NATIONAL BOOK NETWORK

British Library Cataloguing in Publication Information available

Library of Congress Cataloging-in-Publication Data

Names: Kaplan, Susan A., 1951– author. | LeMoine, Genevieve M., author. | Peary-MacMillan Arctic Museum
   & Arctic Studies Center, issuing body.
Title: Peary's Arctic quest : untold stories from Robert E. Peary's North Pole expeditions / Susan A. Kaplan,
   Genevieve M. LeMoine.
Description: Camden, Maine : Down East Books ; Brunswick, Maine : The Peary-MacMillan Arctic Museum,
   [2019] | "Published in cooperation with The Peary-MacMillan Arctic Museum, Bowdoin College,
   Brunswick, Maine." | Includes bibliographical references and index.
Identifiers: LCCN 2018054847 (print) | LCCN 2019009486 (ebook) | ISBN 9781608936441 (electronic) |
   ISBN 9781684750511 (pbk. : alk. paper) | ISBN 9781608936434 (cloth : alk. paper)
Subjects: LCSH: Peary, Robert E. (Robert Edwin), 1856–1920. | Explorers—United States—Biography. | Arctic
   regions—Discovery and exploration. | North Pole—Discovery and exploration.
Classification: LCC G635.P4 (ebook) | LCC G635.P4 K28 2019 (print) | DDC 910.9163/2—dc23
LC record available at https://lccn.loc.gov/2018054847

CONTENTS

Does the world need another book about Robert E. Peary and the North Pole? This was the question we asked ourselves as we embarked on this project more than a decade ago. Our answer was a qualified "yes." Not a book that combs through the events of the 55-day journey over the sea ice in 1909, looking for some lost detail that will definitively prove Peary's location on April 6, 1909. Or one that focuses solely on Peary's motives, constructing a psychological profile to categorize him as a hero, liar, or tragic figure. Rather, we felt it was time to step back and look at his career and his North Pole expedition from a broader perspective. In the long run, whether he, or anyone else, got to the North Pole in the early twentieth century is unknowable.

The impetus for this project was the hundredth anniversary of Peary's 1908–1909 North Pole expedition. Whether you believe he made it to the North Pole or not, this was clearly an event that we at the Peary-MacMillan Arctic Museum felt needed to be acknowledged. In the spring of 2008, we opened a major exhibit, *Northward Over the Great Ice: Robert E. Peary's Quest for the North Pole*. From the earliest planning stages of the project, we decided not to focus on that single, contested achievement, having long since concluded that there is no way to prove whether Peary, Henson, Odaq, Sigluk, Ukkaujaaq, and Iggianguaq were at the North Pole when Peary claimed they were. Far more interesting to us as Arctic anthropologists and archaeologists were some often-neglected aspects of that expedition—the people he chose to employ (and without whom he would have accomplished much less); how he identified or developed, evaluated, and refined the exploration tools and techniques he used; and the positive and negative impacts of his work on the Inughuit community.

Our interest in these topics led us in many different directions. We sought out the unpublished records of expedition members in archives and museums and have also been fortunate to have access to some that have been in family hands for the last 100 years.

Among Peary's often-studied papers at the National Archives and Records Administration in College Park, Maryland, we examined the usual journals and correspondence, but we also paid close attention to things that most other researchers had overlooked, particularly Peary's long obsession with the technological side of his work—designs for improved sledges, snowshoes, stoves, and even ships. Such drawings first appeared before Peary had even been to the Arctic and continued throughout his career. No detail was too small for him if it meant more efficient and more comfortable work. We also looked at the existing papers of the other members of the expedition, some held at our own institution (Bowdoin College) and others scattered around the Northeast. These more personal accounts each give a slightly different perspective on events and include many small details that help bring the North Pole story to life.

In some cases, finding resources was a matter of good luck, such as when we read in a local newspaper that the grandson of George Wardwell, chief engineer on Peary's ship, the SS *Roosevelt*, was visiting family in a town close by and had some of his grandfather's papers. We did not know that Wardwell had kept journals. We were soon to discover that Wardwell was a very consistent diarist, writing every day of his experiences in managing the ship's boilers and engines, and commenting on other activities around the ship (always including what he had for dinner). His account of the 1906 voyage back from the Arctic on a badly damaged vessel, and the events leading up to it, is riveting reading and adds considerably to our understanding of that near-disaster.

Other times we relied on imagination and detective work, including publishing an article in a local newspaper to ask for help in locating a misplaced collection of Wardwell's photographs. The response (and a clue from a Bucksport, Maine, barber) led us on a long trail tracking down a dispersed collection and ultimately to the Castine Historical Society in Castine, Maine, where we combed through "unidentified" files of negatives in the hopes that some of them might prove to be from the North Pole expedition. Miraculously, we found an envelope of negatives that included images of snow-covered landscapes and men wearing polar bear skin pants. These rare Wardwell negatives have now been identified and conserved.

Emma Bonanomi, a curatorial intern at the museum when we were developing the North Pole exhibition, spent months searching for film footage of Matthew Henson, ultimately discovering a rarely seen 1951 interview with him at the age of 85. However, we were not always successful—we continue to look for the 1908–1909 log of the SS *Roosevelt*, last referred to publicly during Peary's congressional hearing in 1911. And we did not stumble on any "smoking gun" that would put to rest the eternal North Pole debate, but we did turn up some interesting material to help flesh out an understanding of Peary's expeditions, the roles played by those who helped him carry out the work, and the impact of those expeditions on the Inughuit with whom he worked.

Archival and museum collections we visited in the course of doing this work include the National Archives and Records Administration, the Academy of Natural Sciences of Drexel University, the American Museum of Natural History, the American Geographical Society, the Explorers Club, the Chemung Valley History Museum, the Maine Historical Society, the Maine State Museum, the Maine Women Writers Collection at the University of New England, the National Geographic Society, and the George J. Mitchell Department of Special Collections and Archives (part of the Bowdoin College Library).

Working in archives and museums is a fundamental part of a project such as this, but to get a sense of some aspects of Peary's career, we are fortunate in having been able to visit many of the places where he worked, although neither of us has been to the North Pole. Being at Bowdoin College, Peary's alma mater, we are of course immersed in the environment in which he spent some of his formative years. Perhaps even more important, we have spent time at his summer home on Eagle Island—his refuge from the world and the place where he was happiest. We have visited Verona Island, Maine, where the only visible remains of the McKay and Dix Shipyard (where the *Roosevelt* was built) are the overgrown ways on which the ship was launched, and nearby Bucksport, where Peary lived in the hotel during the ship's construction. We also have visited the Portland Company property in Portland, Maine, where the *Roosevelt*'s masts and boilers were installed.

Our research has taken us north to St. John's and to Brigus, in Newfoundland and Labrador, where, through the kindness of Catherine Dempsey, then executive director of the Historic Sites Association, we met family members of Robert A. Bartlett, captain of the *Roosevelt*, and relatives of various *Roosevelt* crew members. They opened their homes to us and aided in our search for North Pole expedition–related artifacts, documents, and photographs.

Our quest has taken us farther north, to Battle Harbour, on the coast of Labrador, and the salt loft where Peary gave the first press conference on his return from the North in 1909, and to Iita (Etah) and other locations in northwestern Greenland, home to Inughuit who worked for Peary. In 2011, we were awarded a National Science Foundation, Polar Programs grant to travel to Cape Sheridan, where we spent two weeks examining and evaluating the preservation of the archaeological remains of Peary's 1905–1906 and 1908–1909 expeditions. Parks Canada had done work there in the late 1970s, but we wanted to assess the condition of the archaeological site forty years later and decide whether more extensive research was warranted. We got a lot out of that visit, during which we mapped the tent rings and remains of Peary's crate houses, did some limited test excavations, collected artifacts from the surface of Floeberg Beach, and visited the memorial erected to Ross Marvin. In the end, we decided that further work at the site would not be needed. By being at Cape Sheridan, however, we gained new perspectives on many different aspects of the expedition, from the ways Inughuit women reacted to the challenges of living so far from their home to the sense of foreboding Wardwell often communicated when he wrote about hearing the "ice running" in Nares Strait, for it posed a constant threat to the ship.

Researching this book, then, has been a great adventure, but we were, of course, not alone in our interests and our travels. Intellectually, we owe a great debt to Lyle Dick, who led the way in taking a broader and more critical and considered look at many aspects of Peary's career. We have benefited greatly from his work and from conversations with him over the years. Other scholars and colleagues have also been influential, including Margaret Bertulli, Patricia Erikson, Michael Robinson, Deirdre Stam, and David Stam.

We are also grateful to the extended Peary and Stafford families for welcoming us into their midst and feel fortunate that we met Robert Peary Jr., Peary's son, and Edward Stafford, Peary's grandson, who was instrumental in helping organize the Peary family reunion at Bowdoin College. George Wardwell Jr. generously gave us access to his grandfather's journals and glass lantern slides. Frequently, he would remark, "I knew that stuff in the closet was important!" when we shared with him new insights gleaned from studying the journals and photographs.

We are grateful to the Arctic Museum staff who assisted in research and other work on the exhibit that preceded this book. Anne Witty, then assistant curator, was deeply involved in the research, visiting archives and deploying her skills as a maritime historian to explain to us the details of the *Roosevelt*'s construction. David Maschino worked his magic on the exhibit itself, refining our presentation first through his probing and insightful questions and then in an amazing design and installation of the exhibit. James Tanzer and Steven Bunn each supported the exhibit as well, ensuring that all went smoothly during a major transformation of our galleries and when we opened the exhibit to visitors. Kristi Clifford, then administrative assistant, had the daunting task of arranging our travel and administering various grants, and she also generated the first transcription of George Wardwell's journals. KymNoelle Hopson and Michael Quigley joined the Arctic Museum staff while we were in the process of writing this book and took on various tasks so we could focus on this work. Finally, museum volunteer Mildred Jones worked extensively with the photographs, cataloging and identifying images based on her deep knowledge of the collection developed over more than twenty years.

As a college museum, we have also had the benefit of working with a series of amazing students and interns, including Audrey Amidon, Emma Bonanomi, Eli Bossin, Jennifer Crane, Katie Donlan, Aimée Douglas, Zoe Eddy, Augustus Gilchrist, Rebecca Genauer, Hillary Hooke, Lauren McLaughlin, Ariana Smith, Allison Weisburger, Dana Williams, and David Willner. We are grateful to John Gibbons and Lile Gibbons, who, through two Gibbons fellowships and a Gibbons internship, supported some of the student involvement in our work. We also want to thank the students in the spring 2009 course, "Arctic Exploration in Cultural, Historical, and Environmental Context," for their insightful comments on Arctic exploration literature and their enthusiastic involvement in various North Pole centennial programs.

Foundations that provided collection research and exhibition support include the Museum Loan Network, the Institute of Museum and Library Services (Award MA-02-07-0230-07), the Edgard and Geraldine Feder Foundation, and the Friends of the College Fund. Much of our archival research was supported by a grant from the Kane Lodge Foundation, Inc., which over the years also has supported the preservation of many of the museum's North Pole photograph collections, MacMillan's North Pole photograph album, and some of Peary's instruments. Archaeological fieldwork at Cape Sheridan was supported by the National Science Foundation, Office of Polar Programs Grant ARC-1124811.

The Arctic Museum's Charles Hildreth Endowment funded the conservation of North Pole–related artifacts, and the Russell and Janet Doubleday Endowment provided ongoing program support. We are grateful to the Bowdoin College and greater Brunswick community for their interest in and support of the museum and its programs. We consider it a privilege to work at Bowdoin, where, over almost 160 years, faculty, staff, students, and alumni have been involved in Arctic work. Finally, we wish to express our appreciation to the Qaanaaq and Nunatsiavut communities for their hospitality, the many kindnesses they have extended to us, and their willingness to share their insights with us.

A Note on Names

Peary relied heavily on the indigenous people of northwestern Greenland, who at the time were usually called Eskimos. This name has long since fallen out of favor, and in this book we use the name the people have for themselves: *Inughuit*. This term is a dialectical variant of *Inuit*, specific to the people of the Smith Sound region. Inuit live across the North American Arctic, from Alaska to Greenland, and in Siberia. The groups living in north Alaska, Canada, and Greenland speak a common language, Inuktitut, with regional dialects.

Until the twentieth century, Inuktitut was not a written language, so there were no standardized spellings for people's names or place names. Reading different historic accounts can be challenging, as each author developed their own spelling based on how they understood the pronunciation of a person's name or a geographic place. Since then, spellings have been modernized and standardized, and we use these spellings throughout the book, except in direct quotations. A list of Inughuit mentioned in the text, with the old and new spellings of people's names, can be found at the back of this book. For place names, we also use the modern spellings as found in the national atlas of each country.

Susan A. Kaplan
Genevieve M. LeMoine

Robert E. Peary was an ambitious and charismatic man, with a strong desire to succeed in all his undertakings. Between 1886 and 1909, he made eight trips to the Arctic, some of them multi-year endeavors, altogether spending more than ten years living and working in the North.

Throughout his career he enlisted the support of many people, including his family, financial backers, and loyal expedition members. He learned to rely on the skills of the people who lived their entire lives in the Arctic— the Inughuit men and women of northwestern Greenland—recognizing

Figure 1   Robert E. Peary. This iconic image of Peary at the end of the 1908–1909 expedition has been reproduced many times in many different media. His tired and aged-looking face, surrounded by the thick fur ruff of his parka, brings to mind the many years and extreme sacrifices he made as he worked to accomplish his goal. But there was more to him than dogged determination and a willingness to endure through the most difficult conditions.

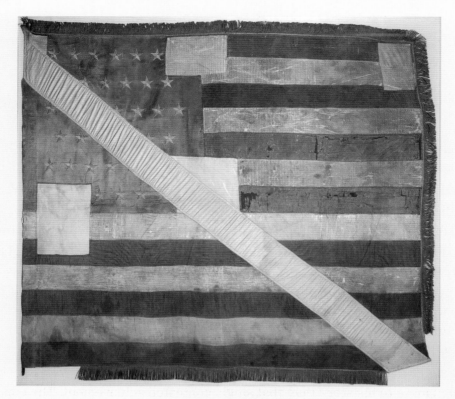

Figure 2   Peary's Flag. On April 6, 1909, Robert E. Peary pulled this silk flag from within his fur parka and unfurled it at the North Pole. His wife, Josephine, kept the flag for many years, donating it to the National Geographic Society in 1955, the year the organization awarded her its Medal of Achievement in recognition of her important role in his work.

that in the Far North their knowledge and technology were superior to anything available farther south. Peary understood that he needed the assistance of all these people to achieve his goals. He also worked ceaselessly to improve his methods of travel and his equipment, always keeping in mind efficiency on the trail as well as the comfort and safety of his men. He was driven by a desire for fame and recognition, but also by a strong nationalistic impulse and a love for life in the Far North.

On April 6, 1909, Peary pulled a fine, hand-sewn silk American flag from within his fur parka and unfurled it at the North Pole, claiming to be the first person to reach that remote spot. Sewn for him by his beloved wife, Josephine Diebitsch Peary, he had carried the flag with him on most of his expeditions; it served as a constant reminder of her support for him through many long, difficult years. Reaching the North Pole was a personal goal for Peary, but he also saw it as a national accomplishment that required American ingenuity and technology to guarantee success over the efforts of other nations.

Patched and tattered, the flag is telling evidence of Peary's long and difficult quest. He carried it with him on his sledging expeditions and cut pieces from it that he left in cairns at key points as a record of his presence in a region. Eventually the flag's missing pieces were replaced with patches. The largest, diagonal patch represents the strip he cut out and left on the sea ice at the North Pole to mark his achievement of being at the northernmost place on Earth.

The flag symbolizes many of the diverse factors that were important to Peary on his long quest to reach that spot: his country, his beloved Josephine, and the many years he had struggled to get to the North Pole. It is, however, silent on the two questions that have dominated all considerations of Peary's work since then: Where exactly was he when he unfurled that flag on April 6 and 7, 1909? And, if he was actually at the North Pole, was he the first person to get there?

Peary's name has become synonymous with the North Pole, but there is much more to his story than that single contested achievement. The controversy over whether he was the first person to reach the North Pole has raged ever since he announced to the world that he had "Stars and stripes nailed to the North pole" in September 1909. Debating these issues clearly has a fascination—more than 100 years later, people are still presenting their vehement opinions as to whether Peary, Frederick Cook, Matthew Henson, or Ralph Plaisted (who snowmobiled to the North Pole in 1968) was the first person to stand at the North Pole. One can, it seems, argue endlessly over sledging times, ice conditions, navigation records (or lack thereof), and any of the myriad factors that argue for or against Peary's claim. Expeditions have tried to replicate Peary's travel methods and travel times, navigators have analyzed his records, and authors have tried to understand his motivations and mental state, but, in the end, there is no way to know absolutely whether he reached the northernmost place on Earth.

Unlike modern polar expeditions, in 1909 Peary could not have produced unassailable proof of his presence at the North Pole. Navigation records could be falsified, as Donald B. MacMillan, an ardent supporter, demonstrated in his 1934 book, *How Peary Reached the Pole*. Unlike the South Pole, which is located on land, the North Pole is located in the Arctic Ocean and is usually covered with floating sea ice. As a result, Peary could not leave a permanent marker documenting his presence at 90° North Latitude. Nor could any independent observer confirm Peary's location. Even the presence of another expert navigator would not have helped cement Peary's claim, as such a person would inevitably be so closely tied to Peary's work that his veracity and impartiality would no doubt have been questioned as well. In the end, it always comes down to Peary's word against those of his detractors.

More than 100 years after the fact, it is time to put these arguments aside and accept that the truth of Peary's claim is unknowable. Ultimately, whether he and his five companions reached precisely 90° North Latitude makes no difference. Apart from the abstract claim of being the first person to stand at that spot, he did not (and could not) make any formal political claim—there is no land at the North Pole to claim. The primary economic benefits of his "first," such as they were, accrued to him, to the news media that fanned the flames of the controversy to sell more news-papers, and, to a lesser extent, to the other members of the expedition, but there were no long-term or more broadly based benefits. Peary was always more concerned with fame than fortune, and reaching the North Pole did little to improve his financial situation. Even today, when the North Pole, including its waters, ocean floor, and that which lies below the sea floor, has become the focus of much media attention, and as nations conduct extensive research missions to establish their right to stake a claim to various segments of the Arctic Ocean, including the North Pole, Peary's achievement (and that of all subsequent claimants) is not consid-ered germane.

The debate surrounding Peary's North Pole achievement has overshad-owed all other aspects of his remarkable career and the accomplishments of his talented crews. Of much greater interest, and the focus of this book, are the multitude of other factors that went into this one journey over the sea ice: the social context of Peary's long quest; the impact it had on the small community of Inughuit in northwestern Greenland; the many years of experimentation, learning, and disappointment that went into design-ing the equipment used on the expedition; and the frequently neglected stories of the remarkable men and women whose support was an essen-tial part of all Peary's expeditions.

In the first three chapters of this book we provide a brief summary of Peary's career, take a detailed look at his last two expeditions, and examine how he went about designing and using equipment, and evaluating his strategies. The following two chapters discuss the large support network upon which he relied, both the Westerners and the Inughuit men and women who were essential to his success. We end with a look at the ways the enduring controversy over Peary's claim to the North Pole has been framed over the last century and a consideration of the fundamental ways in which the Arctic has changed since Peary explored the region.

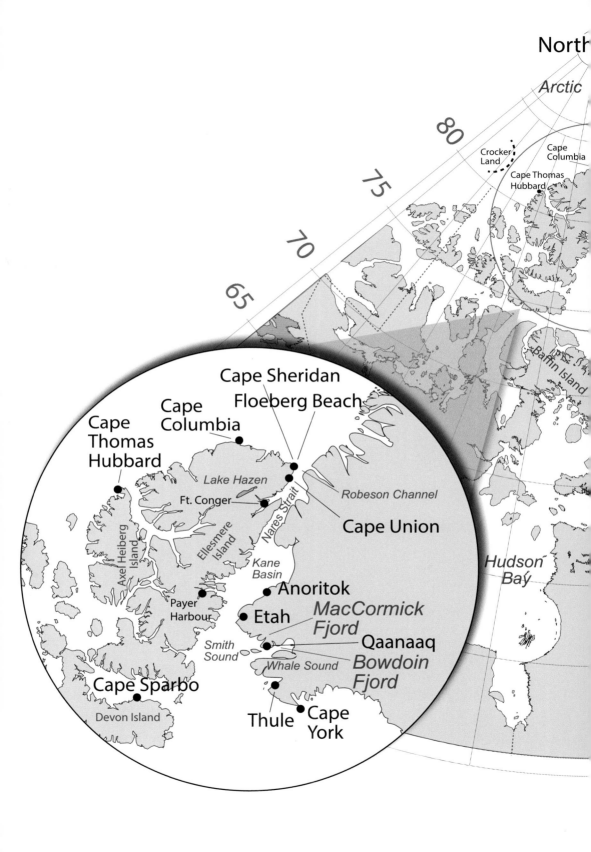

North

Arctic

80

75

70

65

Crocker
Land

Cape
Columbia

Cape Thomas
Hubbard

Baffin Island

*Hudson
Bay*

Cape Sheridan
Floeberg Beach

Cape
Columbia

Cape
Thomas
Hubbard

Lake Hazen

Ft. Conger

Robeson Channel

Cape Union

*Axel Heiberg
Island*

*Ellesmere
Island*

Nares Strait

*Kane
Basin*

Anoritok

Payer
Harbour

Etah

*MacCormick
Fjord*

Qaanaaq

*Smith
Sound*

*Bowdoin
Fjord*

Whale Sound

Cape Sparbo

Devon Island

Thule

Cape
York

Pole

Ocean

Cape Morris Jesup

ape Sheridan

80

Independence Fjord

75

• Anoritok

Etah

70

• Qaanaaq

Greenland

65

hule • Cape York

Baffin Bay

60

Davis Strait

55

50

• Hebron

Labrador

Battle Harbour

Quebec

km

0   400

Map created by KymNoelle Hopson based on OMC map by Martin Weinelt.

1

ROBERT EDWIN PEARY, 1856–1920

> *I would like to acquire a name which would be an*
> *"open sesame" to circles of culture and refinement anywhere,*
> *a name which would make my mother proud and which*
> *would make me feel that I was the peer of anyone I might meet.*

Robert E. Peary wrote these words in a letter to his mother in 1880, when he was 24 years old. He had not yet fixed upon being the first person to reach the North Pole as his route to fame, but within a few years Peary would identify this goal as his chief ambition. Attaining the North Pole became his life's work, ultimately gaining him the national and international prominence he desired.

Peary was born May 6, 1856, in Cresson, Pennsylvania, where his father, Charles Nutter Peary, and uncles had moved to establish a business. He was not quite three years old when his father died of pneumonia, and his mother, Mary Wiley Peary, returned to Maine to raise her only child near her family. She never remarried, instead devoting her life to her son—a decision that was not without its challenges. Mary and "Bertie," as she called him, moved frequently while he was growing up. He attended elementary schools in Cape Elizabeth, Gorham, Topsham, Bethel, and Bridgton before settling in Portland, where he attended Portland High School. Bertie had a mischievous streak, according to his family, but also developed a strong love of the outdoors. He often took long walks, sometimes with friends but more often by himself, and became a keen observer of everything around him. He taught himself taxidermy and became

Figure 3   Charles Nutter Peary and Mary Wiley Peary. This daguerreotype portrait in a leather case with brass mat and gilt frame is believed to show Robert E. Peary's parents, who married in 1854. It was identified as "Grandmother and Grandfather Peary," probably by Robert's daughter Marie Peary.

especially proficient at creating bird mounts. Upon graduating from high school and winning a scholarship to attend Bowdoin College, he sold his taxidermy collection, earning enough money to purchase all his books.

College Student

Peary enrolled at Bowdoin in the fall of 1873. Initially, he did not live on campus like most of the other students, but rather in rooms he and his

Figure 4   Bertie Peary, Age Three. "Bertie" Peary was only three years old when this photograph was taken. Mary Wiley Peary raised her son alone, and although he was often naughty, he was always devoted to her. As a young man, he relied on her advice and wrote to her frequently when he was away from home.

mother had rented in Brunswick. At Bowdoin he continued to develop his interests in science and natural history. He majored in civil engineering, graduating second in his class. He was hardworking and gifted and was considered the most successful graduate of this short-lived college program. In letters to friends and in his diary, he wrote with pleasure about his various successes in and out of the classroom. His careful observations, attention to detail, and love of problem solving—characteristics that would become important to his later success—all blossomed while he was at Bowdoin.

Bowdoin provided Peary with a good education, and he formed some lasting friendships. Rather surprisingly, given his training, energy, and ambition, he did not move immediately into a career. Instead, he and his

Figure 5   Extracurricular Activities. Although often considered a loner, Peary was involved in college extracurricular activities. He was a member of Delta Kappa Epsilon, which he joined in his freshman year. In addition, he served on the editorial committee of the student yearbook, *Bugle*, and was on the Committee of Arrangements for Ivy Day. He wrote the ode for Ivy Day in 1876 and also had the honor of planting the actual ivy. According to the *Bowdoin Orient*, "A neat, marble tablet in the form of an ivy leaf, affixed to the wall of the Chapel nearby, is to distinguish it from all which may be planted hereafter."

Figure 6   Snowy Owl. Peary's love of the outdoors continued during his college years, and he often went on long hikes, sometimes collecting specimens to continue his hobby of taxidermy. Bowdoin College still has mounts of every owl species found in Maine that Peary created while he was a student.

Admiral Robert E. Peary

Figure 7   Coming of Age. Peary graduated second in his class from Bowdoin with a degree in civil engineering in 1877.

mother took up residence in the small town of Fryeburg in western Maine. There was no call for civil engineers in the small town, so Peary drew on his youthful energy to make work for himself. Once again he took up taxidermy and sold mounts, and he also made some money training horses. In addition, he decided to create an accurate and detailed map of the town.

In the end, this map served multiple purposes. Producing it kept him busy and his hard-earned engineering and drafting skills fresh, and the map itself was instrumental in landing him a position as a draftsman with the Coast and Geodetic Survey in Washington, D.C., where he moved in the summer of 1879 to begin his professional life in earnest. He worked for the Survey for two years but soon found the work dull and became eager to do something different. In the fall of 1881, after taking a grueling series of exams, he was appointed a U.S. Navy civil engineer. He would remain a member of the navy for the rest of his career, although he was often on leave.

Lieutenant Peary

It was through the navy that Peary got his first real taste of exploration, not in the Arctic but in the tropics. In the winter of 1885 he spent three

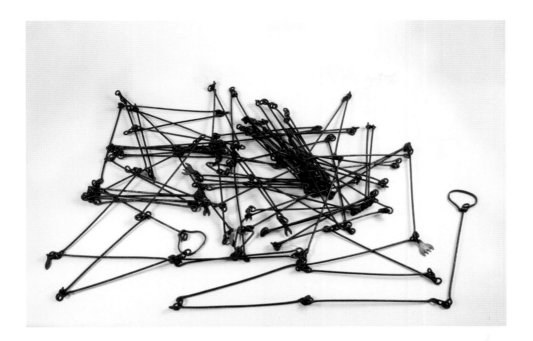

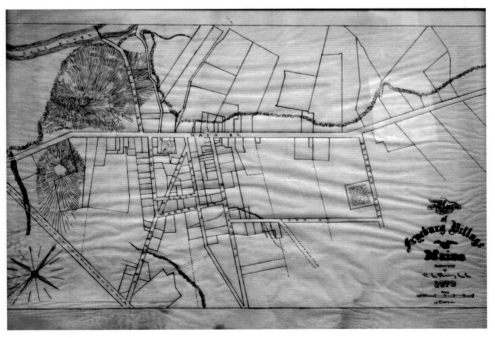

Figures 8 and 9   Setting Out. Peary and his mother moved to Fryeburg, Maine, after his graduation from college. Although he did not find engineering work, Peary practiced his draftsmanship by mapping the village. He used this 100-foot engineer's chain to measure distances.

Figure 10   Far from Home. Peary wrote about his Nicaragua work in his diary: "Scarcely a place where fifty feet could be gained without cutting or clearing away a log or lifting the boats over one . . . all the men and myself as well, constantly [in water] to our knees and waists and even necks, cutting, lifting, pulling, pushing, swimming."

months in Nicaragua surveying a section of land covered with dense jungle and extensive swamps for a proposed canal to link the Atlantic and Pacific oceans. The leader of this expedition, Aniceto Garcia Menocal, praised Peary for his determination in the face of many hardships, though neither he nor Peary realized how well it had prepared him for the next phase of his career.

Peary's interest in Arctic exploration grew in the 1880s as he read everything he could find on the topic, nurturing the idea that he might be the first person to reach the North Pole. In the fall of 1885, he wrote a detailed and surprisingly prescient memorandum outlining his ideas about how to successfully reach the North Pole: "The only way is to lie in wait at some favorable point + watch season after season ready to take advantage of a favorable one, + believe me there will come that season when the fortunate man waiting on the verge of the unknown region can speed away to the Pole even as the Polaris sped through Melville B. + up Smith Sd." Many of the key elements of this statement were included in plans he put into action two decades later. Based on his reading, he realized that to survive in the North, one should follow Inuit practices, adopting their style of clothing and modes of transportation. Also, he recognized the capriciousness of Arctic weather and sea ice conditions. Before he ever set foot in the Far North, he had developed a clear idea of what he wanted to accomplish and how he would go about doing it. This memorandum may have marked a turning point in Peary's career. Yes, his work for the navy was successful, and at times challenging, but he had greater ambitions.

EXPLORATION LITERATURE

Peary read a wide range of Arctic exploration literature, which was of great popular interest in the nineteenth century. Arctic exploration was once a preoccupation largely of the British navy, which was seeking the Northwest Passage. By the 1850s, American explorers had joined the fray and were venturing north, ostensibly to assist in the search for Sir John Franklin's lost expedition, but also to seek the "Open Polar Sea." The explorers wrote books about their expeditions. Of particular interest was American explorer Elisha Kent Kane's *Arctic Explorations*, published in 1857, describing his recent expedition to Smith Sound. It was one of the most popular books of its day, with more than 200,000 copies sold in the first two years after it was published. Peary was also influenced by the work of Captain George Nares of the Royal Navy, who wintered his ship *Alert* at Floeberg Beach on northern Ellesmere Island in 1875–1876, and Frederick Schwatka, an American who led an expedition to northern Canada to recover information about the lost Franklin expedition in 1878. Unlike previous explorers, Schwatka traveled with Inuit guides using dog sledges, covering about 2,700 miles in 11 months. Peary saw this as a key American innovation and a model for future Arctic expeditions.

With characteristic care and attention to detail, Peary began to plan how he would achieve his goal. His first step was to undertake a summer trip to the Greenland ice cap, to test his affinity for northern work. Using skis and snowshoes and dragging food and equipment on light sledges behind them, he and Christian Maigaard, a young Danish man he had met in Greenland, traveled for two weeks, covering 100 miles before turning back with only six days of provisions left. Though the men encountered difficulties on the trip, they ventured farther onto the ice cap than anyone before them. Peary caught the Arctic bug and was determined to return to Greenland and cross the ice cap. Before launching his next expedition, however, two important people came into his life.

Figure 11 Josephine Cecilia Diebitsch Peary. Josephine Diebitsch Peary was a remarkable woman. She was born near Washington, D.C., in 1863, at the height of the Civil War. Her parents had emigrated from Germany, and she was raised speaking German as well as English. Prior to her marriage to Robert E. Peary in 1888, she worked for the Census Bureau and the Smithsonian Institution. As Peary's wife, she was his strongest and most loyal supporter and an effective fundraiser.

Josephine Diebitsch first met Peary at a dance in Washington, D.C., in 1882. After a long courtship, they were married in the summer of 1888. Josephine was a remarkable and resourceful woman, and it is safe to say that without her, Peary would have had a much more difficult time accomplishing his goals.

Matthew Henson came to Peary's attention in 1887. Peary had been given responsibility for carrying out all survey work for the proposed canal through Nicaragua and, as part of his preparation, was looking for a valet. Henson, already a seasoned traveler, was then working in a haberdashery in Washington, D.C., and was recommended to Peary by the owner of the shop. Henson acquitted himself well on that trip—so well that Peary hired him again to go on his next Arctic expedition, not as a valet but as an assistant.

Throughout the 1880s Peary was preparing for a career as an Arctic explorer, and by the end of the decade the pieces were mostly in place. He had distinguished himself in his work for the navy and gained experience

Figure 12   Matthew Henson. Matthew Henson was born in Maryland in 1866. At age 12, he became a cabin boy on the *Katie Hines* and sailed throughout the world. He was Peary's valet on a Nicaragua survey- ing expedition and later became Peary's most trusted assistant on seven Arctic expeditions.

in the North. He had met and married Josephine, a woman his equal in determination and courage, and he had found in Henson an able assis- tant. After his second season in Nicaragua, Peary turned his attention to funding his return to Greenland. An invitation to deliver a lecture at the Brooklyn Institute gave him an opportunity to get the word out about his ambitions and ideas for an expedition, and by early 1891 he had the support of a number of institutions and enough money to proceed with planning.

Plans in Place

The 1891 expedition had nothing to do with the North Pole—Peary's goal was to explore northern Greenland by way of the interior. He explained, "It is like exploring an atoll around the margin of the placid central lagoon, instead of along the outer shore, through reefs and breakers."

This expedition would answer key geographical questions, such as whether Greenland was an island, and test the viability of using northern Greenland as a route to the North Pole. His plan was to charter a ship that would leave him and his small party in Whale Sound, in northwestern Greenland, before returning south. The vessel would pick them up the following summer. During the year, the expedition party would construct a house to use as a base, pay Inughuit women to make them appropriate clothes, and hire local Inughuit men to teach them how to drive dog-drawn sledges. After a winter spent preparing, the team would set off across the ice cap, where no one had yet ventured.

ICE TYPES

Peary's extensive reading and first trip to the inland ice covering much of Greenland had taught him a bit about the differences between the surfaces of the Greenland ice cap and the frozen oceans. Both surfaces pose their own challenges for traveling and require different equipment and skills.

The Greenland ice cap is for the most part relatively smooth, but the edge can be treacherous. There the ice flows slowly outward, and as it does, it cracks. These cracks, known as crevasses, are deep, narrow fissures into which people and dogs can fall. Often snow forms weak bridges over the cracks, effectively disguising them, creating hazardous traveling conditions. Getting onto and off the ice cap is the most dangerous part of any journey across it.

The sea ice poses many dangers of its own. A frozen ocean is not a flat, uniform expanse of ice. Close to land, sea ice can form a relatively smooth and stable platform for travel. This is called fast ice, and it is anchored to the land. It typically forms in the winter and melts again each summer and can be up to six feet thick. Additionally, in some places an "ice foot" forms. It is a narrow fringe of ice at the high tide line that can persist even into the summer. Beyond the fast ice is the pack ice, floating on the ocean. Until recently, much of this ice was many years old and up to 16 feet thick. Pack ice can be relatively flat, but it is often interrupted by pressure ridges, huge piles of broken ice that pile up when winds, currents, and tides move the ice in different directions and pieces raft up on one another. Both pack ice and the fast ice can also be interrupted by cracks in the ice, called leads, which expose open water even in the depths of winter. Pressure ridges and leads are significant barriers for anyone traveling across the sea ice.

In broad strokes, this is how the expedition proceeded, but things did not always go smoothly. A minor scandal arose even before the party left the United States: Josephine had decided to accompany her husband, a radical decision for the time that was met with public disapproval. Just before the ship carrying the party reached Whale Sound, Peary broke his leg in a shipboard accident. Overall, however, the expedition went very much as planned. The party made contact with the Inughuit, hired men to teach them the intricacies of driving dog teams and other skills, and paid women to sew them warm fur clothing. The journey over the ice cap was grueling, but Peary and Eivind Astrup did reach land at the northern end of Greenland, sighting Independence Fjord on July 4, 1892. The end of the expedition was marred by the tragic disappearance of one of its members, John Verhoeff, who had ventured off on his own just before they were to depart from Greenland; despite days of searching, he was never found.

Once back home, Peary, who had learned that a bit of showmanship would attract the attention of prospective donors, immediately set out on an ambitious lecture tour to raise funds for a new expedition. He took Matthew Henson along to model Arctic clothing, demonstrate some of the equipment, and manage the sledge dogs brought back from Greenland. Peary earned $20,000 that winter, enough for his small family to live on (he had extended his leave from the navy), with some left over to fund an expedition.

He and Josephine returned to Greenland in 1893. Again their plans raised a stir, for this time Josephine was pregnant. They were accompanied by a nurse/midwife to assist Josephine, who gave birth to her first child, Marie Ahnighito Peary, on September 12, 1893, in the expedition headquarters known as Anniversary Lodge on the shore of Bowdoin Fjord.

Figure 13 Peary with a Broken Leg. In mid-July 1891, Peary was immobilized for weeks by his broken leg, leaving him to supervise the early work of the expedition from his bed. He was able to walk with crutches in September, but it was October before he could walk unaided. Yet he never considered abandoning his plans.

Figure 14   Navy Cliff. Standing on this promontory on July 4, 1892, Peary was the first Euro-American to see the rugged coast of northern Greenland. He named the spot on which he stood "Navy Cliff" and, inspired by the date, called the long inlet before him Independence Fjord. He later wrote, "Before me, the warm red-brown landscape wavered and trembled in the yellow light; behind me, towered the blinding white slopes of the ice. Beneath my feet, the stones were bare even of lichens, and had a dry, grey look, as if they were the bones of a dead world."

With ambitious plans for exploring far northern Greenland, Peary and seven others (including Henson and Dr. Frederick Cook, the physician who had set Peary's leg on the previous expedition) set out across the ice cap in the late winter of 1894. However, they encountered so many difficulties that they had to turn back long before reaching Independence Fjord. The only bright spot was a brief journey to the south that summer to identify the location of the iron meteorite fragments that local people had been using for generations, fashioning pieces they chipped off into knives.

In late summer, the *Falcon* arrived to take the team home. Peary, however, was not ready to give up his investigation of northern Greenland. He decided to stay another winter, and two men, Matthew Henson and Hugh Lee, volunteered to stay with him. Everyone else, including Josephine and baby Marie, returned to the United States. A young Inughuit teenager, Eqariusaq (called "Miss Bill" by the Pearys), accompanied Josephine, with plans to spend a year in the United States.

Peary, Henson, and Lee reached Independence Fjord the next spring, but just barely. They and their dogs were near starvation when, luckily, the men shot a muskox. They did not have the resources to do any further exploring, so they turned back. The trip to Bowdoin Fjord was equally hard. They reached Anniversary Lodge with only one dog, the rest having been eaten—first by the other dogs, and then by the men.

That summer, when the *Kite* arrived to take them home, Peary had the ship stop at Cape York, where he retrieved two of the meteorite fragments he had seen the previous summer. Known to the Inughuit as "dog" and "woman," together they weighed more than 6,000 pounds. The largest piece, known as the "tent" (renamed "Ahnighito" by Peary), was too massive to move, but Peary (perhaps with the assistance of his brother-in-law, Emil Diebitsch, who had sailed north on the *Kite*) hatched a plan to retrieve it as well.

Emil's presence on the *Kite* was a surprise and a bit of a disappointment for Peary, as he had hoped that Josephine and Marie would be on board. Josephine had chosen to stay home this time, however, having spent the previous winter raising money to charter the ship to retrieve her husband. Eqariusaq, having spent a year living with Josephine and Marie, was on board and happily reunited with her family, although by all accounts they did not believe many of the tales she told of her adventures.

The next few years were relatively uneventful. Peary returned north only in the summers in 1896 and 1897, trying to retrieve the large iron meteorite he had named "Ahnighito." Finally, in 1897, with the help of

Figure 15 "Ahnighito" Meteorite Being Raised from the Hold. It took all the engineering skills of Peary and his brother-in-law Emil Diebitsch to move the massive "Ahnighito" meteorite onto a ship that could carry it to New York. Eventually Josephine was able to sell this and the two smaller pieces he carried home in 1895 to the American Museum of Natural History, where they remain on view today.

Figure 16 New York Inughuit with Albert Operti. Nuttak (Eqariusaq's father), with his wife Atangana and their daughter Aviaq, Qisuk and his son Minik, and Uisaakkassak, with the artist Albert Operti, on board the *Hope* en route to New York in 1897. Unlike Eqariusaq's uneventful trip, this one was disastrous. Within months of arriving in New York, Nuttak, Atangana, Aviaq, and Qisuk had died of respiratory diseases. Uisaakkassak survived and returned to Greenland the next summer, but orphaned Minik was adopted by a museum staff member and raised in New York. Their tragic story has been told elsewhere.

Emil, he succeeded. Many years later, Josephine sold the meteorites to the American Museum of Natural History in New York City, where they remain on exhibit. However, the meteorites were not all he brought back. Anthropologist Franz Boas, of the American Museum of Natural History, had asked Peary if he could find an Inughuit man who would be willing to travel south to spend a winter working with Boas and his colleagues. Boas had spent a year living with Inuit on Baffin Island in the 1880s and was interested in learning about other Inuit groups. Peary was happy to oblige, though he brought not one man but six people.

A New Approach

Peary had to reassess his North Pole strategy. The trips over the ice cap had demonstrated that this was not a practical route to the Pole. Therefore, he returned to his original idea, first formulated in 1885, that the best route north was through Smith Sound and Kane Basin. He resolved to travel with a small team and establish a base camp where he could wait for a favorable season to make the trip across the Polar Sea to the Pole. So began four harrowing years, 1898–1902, during which he, Matthew Henson, and Dr. Thomas Dedrick lived mostly on Ellesmere Island, as Peary made multiple unsuccessful attempts to reach the Pole.

The challenges they faced are too numerous to document here. This is the expedition on which an underpowered ship failed to penetrate the ice as far north as Peary had planned, putting them 250 miles south of where they had hoped to establish their base camp. Other problems followed. Peary's feet were so badly frostbitten that Dr. Dedrick had to amputate most of his toes. Henson found an Inughuit wife, Elatu, only to lose her to an incurable disease.

In the summer of 1900, Josephine chartered a ship to take her north so she could convince Peary to come home; she subsequently found herself frozen in at Payer Harbour, Ellesmere Island, while Peary, unaware of her presence, wintered more than 200 miles north, at Fort Conger. She carried the sad news that their second child, a girl born after Peary left, had died before her first birthday. At Payer Harbour, Josephine discovered that her husband had an Inughuit wife who had borne him a child. When she and Peary were finally reunited that summer, they somehow overcame that challenge to their marriage, but she was unsuccessful in convincing him to return home, and he remained in the North for another winter. All to no avail. Peary made a final attempt at the Pole in the spring of 1902 and achieved a new farthest north record, but impossible ice conditions forced him to turn back at 84°16'27" North. He was bitterly disappointed, noting that at age 46 he was "too old for this kind of work." He wrote in his journal, "My dream of sixteen years is ended. I close the book and turn to others less interesting, but better suited for my years."

Once Peary was reunited with his family and home again, he got over his disappointment. While he felt that he had failed to achieve his goal, others saw much about him to admire. He was elected president of the American Geographical Society and awarded gold medals by both the Scottish and the French geographical societies. He also had a number of wealthy and powerful supporters, including Morris K. Jesup, Herbert Bridgman, and even President Theodore Roosevelt. While he had been in the North, Jesup and Bridgman, along with other wealthy businessmen, had formed the Peary Arctic Club expressly to support Peary's work.

Ultimately, Peary was not able to let go of his goals, and he resolved once again to try to reach the North Pole. His own persistent nature played a role here, as did his ability to learn from his mistakes. Now, he turned to his wealthy and influential supporters to further his cause. What he really needed was his own ship, a vessel that could be forced through pack ice to put a team as far north as possible. The vessel would remain in the Arctic through the winter to serve as a headquarters for the expedition. Expedition members would live on the ship in relative comfort through the fall and winter before sledging north the following spring.

Over the next five years, Peary made his final two trips to the Arctic aboard the SS *Roosevelt*, a vessel built to his specifications. Peary's career as an explorer essentially ended after he reached the North Pole on April 6, 1909. He announced his success to the world at the earliest opportunity, from a wireless station on the southern coast of Labrador, but he was too late—Frederick Cook, the physician who had set his broken leg, once a colleague, was now a rival American explorer. Days before Peary announced his achievement, Cook declared that he had reached the Pole one year earlier. The controversy over which man had been to the Pole first consumed much of Peary's later life.

Lasting Fame

Peary was bitterly disappointed that his hard-won success was contested, but he had powerful supporters on his side and was eventually declared the discoverer of the North Pole, achieving the lasting fame he had wished

Figure 17   Distinguished Retirement. Upon his return from the North Pole in 1909, Peary was appointed rear admiral of the U.S. Navy. In spite of many disappointments and setbacks, he had finally achieved fame. His name and his accomplishments were known around the world. In retirement, he turned his attention to other matters. Most significantly, he developed an interest in flight and was an early advocate for military aviation.

for as a young man. The years immediately after his return from the North were filled with celebratory dinners, lecture tours, and award ceremonies. He was promoted first to captain in 1910, then to rear admiral in 1911 when he retired from active duty.

More satisfying than accolades, however, was the time he finally had to spend with his family and at his beloved summer home on Eagle Island in Casco Bay, Maine. Peary had purchased the island in 1881 with money from his first real job. In 1904, he and Josephine built a small summer cottage there, and it became a refuge for them and their two children (Marie and Robert Jr.). Josephine was on Eagle Island in September 1909 when she received Peary's telegram announcing his North Pole success, and in the following years the couple spent as much time there as possible.

Although showing signs of the strain of his years in the Arctic, Peary was still fit, energetic, and as full of curiosity as ever. Ever the innovator, he recognized the value of flight for both civil and military purposes. He was a strong and vocal proponent of military aviation for many years, foreseeing its growing importance and actively working to improve the nation's civil defense as the First World War loomed. He was chairman of the National Aerial Coastal Patrol Commission, a group formed to promote the establishment of a series of bases along the U.S. coast to conduct aerial surveillance. He traveled widely, speaking on this subject, and

Figure 18   **At Eagle Island.** Eagle Island was Peary's "promised land." Even while he was on the sea ice, his thoughts turned to his summer home, and he sometimes jotted down ideas for improving the cottage. Friends noted that Peary was most himself when he was on the island.

Figure 19   Peary in Flying Costume. Peary's interest in flight consumed much of his time and energy after he retired. Here he models a sheepskin flying suit, probably of his design, apparently demonstrating its comfort and functionality.

wrote many letters and articles urging the government to invest in military aviation. His vision went beyond the immediate threat of war. He was convinced that investment in military aviation would pay off in times of peace, writing that "the money and effort expended on our air service will all count toward a great peace air service . . . the carrying of mails; the transportation of passengers and express material; the lifesaving patrol of our coasts."

In those years Peary did not often mention the benefits of flight for exploration, but they were certainly on his mind. In 1918, he and Robert Bartlett, who had served as captain of the *Roosevelt*, announced ambitious plans for a major expedition involving three research stations around the Arctic Ocean, multiple aircraft, and multiple ships. The goal was to map and study the huge blank spot on maps north of Alaska all the way to the Pole. Sadly, this was never to be. Peary had been diagnosed with "pernicious anemia," and although blood transfusions helped for a while, he eventually succumbed to the disease. He died on February 20, 1920, at his home in Washington, D.C., and was buried with great fanfare in Arlington National Cemetery.

2

REACHING FOR THE POLE: THE 1905–1906 AND 1908–1909 EXPEDITIONS

In July 1905, the SS *Roosevelt* steamed out of New York Harbor on its maiden voyage to the Arctic. Robert Peary, with a carefully selected group of assistants, was setting forth on what he hoped would be his final attempt to reach the North Pole. Building on his years of experience, and having learned many hard lessons, he had done everything in his power to make this trip a success. The only things he left to chance were those he could not control, of which the most important were the weather and the condition of the sea ice. Either of these things could mean failure once again.

After multiple unsuccessful attempts to reach the North Pole, Peary had developed a new approach, grounded in his years of experience in the North but now on a grander scale. The most important change was this new vessel, the SS *Roosevelt*. With the daring young captain Robert A. Bartlett at the helm, Peary was confident that he could gain an important edge: placing him and his team, with all their equipment and supplies, farther north than ever before. This would situate them closer to their goal, reducing the length of their trip and the distance they would need to move supplies. The ship would be frozen in for the winter, a comfortable base from which to work and a way home for the team when the work was done.

A second significant change was the size of the team. On his earlier attempts Peary had worked with a small team composed of himself, Henson, and a few Inughuit men. This time he devised a more elaborate plan, in which some teams would precede him over the sea ice on the trip to the Pole, breaking trail and laying in caches of supplies that would allow him to travel much of the way along a well-trodden path, unburdened by the need to carry all the food his men and dogs would require for the trip there and back. If the weather and ice cooperated, these two changes would make it possible for him to reach his goal.

From the start, things did not always go according to plan. Trouble began immediately, when the ship caught fire due to the proximity of reinforcing beams to the boilers. One set of boilers ran dry and was damaged, but the fire was quickly extinguished. Peary makes little of these events in his book *Nearest the Pole*, but his chief engineer, George Wardwell, was less sanguine. In his personal journal Wardwell reports a number of other fires in subsequent days, along with the need to cut away some of the beams and sheath others in iron to protect them. Two of the three boilers were out of commission for weeks, and even when he had finally repaired them they continued to be finicky and unreliable—so much so that they were deemed "volcanic" by the firemen and Wardwell named them Pele and Vesuvius.

Figure 20 *Erik and Roosevelt* **in Foulke Fjord.** The *Roosevelt* was so heavily buttressed that there was not enough room in the hold for all the coal it would need to carry to get back home again. In both 1905–1906 and 1908–1909, the *Erik* carried coal to Etah and left a supply there. In 1905, the supply was inadequate, contributing to the *Roosevelt*'s difficult journey home in 1906.

After an otherwise uneventful trip to Greenland, the team stopped at a number of Inughuit communities to hire families to work for the expedition. The *Roosevelt* also spent a few days at Etah, where they took on coal that a second vessel, the *Erik*, had carried north for them.

Then the real struggle began. On August 16, Bartlett steamed north through the ice-choked waters of Smith Sound, Kane Basin, and Nares Strait. For weeks they battled the ice, much to Peary and Bartlett's delight.

Figure 21 *Roosevelt* **in the Ice.** In *Nearest the Pole*, Peary vividly described the *Roosevelt* engaging with the ice: "The *Roosevelt* fought like a gladiator, turning, twisting, straining with all her force, smashing her full weight against the heavy floes whenever we could get room for a rush, and rearing upon them like a steeplechaser taking a fence. Ah, the thrill and tension of it, the lust of battle, which crowded days of ordinary life into one."

Finally, on September 5, Bartlett piloted the *Roosevelt* into a thin strip of open water below Cape Sheridan, two miles north of the spot where Captain George Nares of the Royal Navy had frozen in the *Alert* in 1875—a new farthest north point for a ship. They were in a shallow bay that to all appearances left them exposed to the dangerous grinding pack ice in the narrow channel between Ellesmere Island and Greenland. Strong currents drove thick pack ice through the channel even in the depths of winter. But Peary and Bartlett knew, thanks to Nares, that the bay was protected by an underwater shoal. The thickest, most dangerous floes would ground on the shoal, forming a barrier to protect the ship. Only once did the driving pack seriously threaten the ship, in mid-September, before the fast ice had formed, when the incoming tide brought the towering remains of a pressure ridge right up to the *Roosevelt*. Peary describes this near-disaster in stirring language:

[F]or a minute or so, which seemed an age, the pressure was terrific. The *Roosevelt*'s ribs and interior bracing cracked like the discharge of musketry; the deck amidships bulged up several inches, while the main rigging hung slack and the masts and rigging shook as in a violent gale.

Figure 22   Floeberg Beach in 2011. The shallow bay at Floeberg Beach offered some protection for the *Roosevelt*. Here, the authors, conducting archaeological research at Cape Sheridan in 2011, are seen examining the remains of one of the crate houses Peary's team constructed in 1908.

The danger passed with the ship unscathed, but as a result of this scare the team began moving more supplies from the ship to shore for safety in case the ship was crushed. Peary and Bartlett also used dynamite to destroy some of the thick floes around the ship, causing extensive damage to the stern and engine room. Chief engineer Wardwell described the effects of these efforts in his journal and spent many subsequent days repairing the damage. In the following months, Wardwell often remarked on the terrifying sound of the pack ice running in the strait. In February, he reported that he "went out to the edge of the running ice today it was moving South about a mile an hour. It is heavy ice and has been rafted up on some big sheet somewhere and broken off and crowded up. Piled up 30 or 40 feet some of it." Despite the apparent danger, the *Roosevelt* remained safe that winter, and again in 1908–1909.

WARDWELL ON DAMAGE DUE TO BLASTING

Wardwell wrote in his journal, September 16:

The ice came rushing in about 10.30 last night and crowded us up on top of a big floe raised us up about 6 feet and the deck 3 or 4 inches and we worked all night getting provisions coal, stoves etc. on the ice, in case the ship got crushed we would have something to eat but she came back all right about 3 oclock in the morning and then they went at work blasting fired one charge under the stern and raised the tanks broke a pipe and I went up and told them what it had done and thought they were getting a little close but they thought it was all right So they put in another charge raised the Engine about an inch broke a piece out of the bed broke two more pipes raised the tanks raised the Condenser about 4 inches pull[ed] two 4 inch pipes with threads on them out broke one 8 inch pipe 1" thick blew an Excentric [sic] strap weighing 200 lbs half across the Engine room shifted the air pump from the foundation blew the floor up and the engine bed about 1 inch unhooked the chain fell over the engine fell down. broke 4 steps out of the upper engines ladder threw all the oil boxes out of the thrush bearing blew all the pipe fittings across the Engineroom broke the glass in the skylight broke a pipe in the air pump and the Indication pipe in the Engine broke the pipe under the air pump that runs to the tank I dont know of anything else it broke. cant tell until I get steam on the Engine couldnt turn the wheel when the ice was coming in havent tried it since they didnt fire anymore after the things went in the air it made the ship leak a little if it had been a common ship there would been a hole as big as a hogshead as it was it splintered things up some the Scotch boiler jumped up about 2" and the Almys went dancing around it was a close call.

Figure 23 Women Sewing on Board the *Roosevelt*. Inughuit women were an essential part of Peary's expeditions, although they received little attention for their crucial work. Their most important role was to sew clothing, not only for their families but also for Peary and his men. The women lived in houses on shore while the *Roosevelt* was frozen into the ice at Cape Sheridan. They accompanied their husbands on some sledge journeys, but none went on the trip to the Pole.

Once at Cape Sheridan, the real work of the expedition began. The fall was devoted to preparations. Newcomers to the Arctic, such as Peary's chief assistant Ross Marvin and Dr. Louie J. Wolf, had to learn essential survival skills. Teams of Inughuit hunters set out to hunt for game to feed both people and dogs, or they worked with Matthew Henson constructing dog-drawn sledges. In addition to tending to all their other family responsibilities, women sewed clothing for the expedition men.

Everyone worked through the darkest part of the winter, and on February 19 the first team set out for the trip to the Pole. In addition to Henson, Bartlett, Marvin, and Wolf, Peary had two of the ship's firemen, Charles Clark and Matthew Ryan, as members of the sledging teams. Peary's plan was to have teams departing one day apart and then hop-scotching forward, moving supplies along the trail, with Henson's party (Panikpak, Piugattoq, and Sipsu) often in the lead. Some teams, having established caches on the sea ice, returned to land to pick up more supplies and move them up the trail.

From the beginning, the ice conditions were difficult. In fact, the winter of 1905–1906 was unusually warm, creating dangerous ice conditions that

Figure 24 Teams Working in Challenging Conditions. On the way to the Pole, the team in the lead created or broke a trail, traveling for 12–18 hours before stopping to build an igloo, have dinner, and sleep. The next morning they would be off again. Following teams would reuse the igloos, building more only if necessary. Sometimes they would use ice as a raft to transport dogs and sledges across open leads. Sledging back to land, the men followed their old trail as much as possible. Often on the way back they were able to travel twice as far each day than they had on the way up, stopping at one igloo for lunch before hitting the trail again to stop at a second igloo for the night.

ultimately led to the failure of this attempt. Leads opened up, sometimes running right through the igloos where men slept. New pressure ridges rose, and the trail was often disrupted as the ice moved.

In late March, all progress came to a halt for a week, as the parties breaking trail waited for a particularly wide lead, referred to as "The Big Lead" (or, as Peary named it, the "Hudson River"), to close. When it did, Peary and Henson were able to cross with their teams. They made good progress for a few days, but then the travelers faced another six-day delay due to weather. These days of strong winds opened up the Big Lead again, preventing Marvin and his team from crossing with essential supplies for the rest of the journey. This development left Peary with more people and fewer supplies than he needed, forcing him to abandon his plan to reach the Pole and instead settle for a new farthest north record. On April 21, after a series of long days, traveling sometimes thirty miles or more, they reached 87° 6' North—a new record.

By this time the Inughuit men were becoming concerned about the state of the ice, worried that they would not be able to get safely back to land.

Odaq, as he recounted to Knud Rasmussen some years later, spoke to Peary about their worries and said that if Peary wanted to go on, most of the men should be sent home, and he would stay with Peary to continue the journey. Peary did not need to take Odaq up on his generous and brave offer, however. He, too, was concerned about their safety and, satisfied with a new record, had decided they should all turn back. Then began the most difficult part of the journey.

A HARD DAY'S WORK

Breaking trail was hard work. Often teams would wield their axes to cut a trail through jumbled ice, and then they would help the dogs pull the heavily laden sledges, maneuvering them through the tangle of ice. The men ate two meals a day, both consisting of half a pound of pemmican, half a pound of hard tack, and a mug of hot tea. Pemmican is a mixture of dry meat, suet, and raisins. Hard tack is a very basic and long-lasting hard cracker. The dogs also ate a type of pemmican and were allotted one pound per day.

In later years, Peary described his feelings about this diet:

I recall innumerable marches in bitter temperatures when men and dogs had been worked to the limit and I reached the place for camp feeling as if I could eat my weight of anything. When the pemmican ration was dealt out, and I saw my little half-pound lump, about as large as the bottom third of an ordinary drinking-glass, I have often felt a sullen rage that life should contain such situations. By the time I had finished the last morsel I would not have walked round the completed igloo for anything or everything that the St. Regis, the Blackstone, or the Palace Hotel could have put before me.

Strong persistent winds had dogged them for weeks, causing the ice on which they were traveling to drift eastward. Peary chose to head not toward Ellesmere Island, where they had left land, but instead to Greenland, which was now the nearest land. Time was not on their side. They needed to get off the pack ice as quickly as possible, but luck was not with them. They came to the Big Lead, now a solidly frozen jumble of ice that they crossed only with great difficulty. Beyond it a new "Big Lead" had opened, christened by a less hopeful Peary as "The Styx." This they eventually managed to cross by sliding carefully across very thin ice while wearing snowshoes, the toes of their boots sometimes breaking

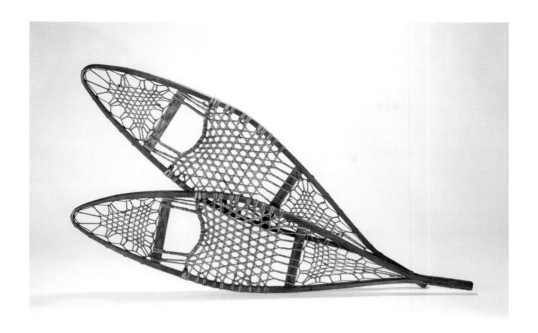

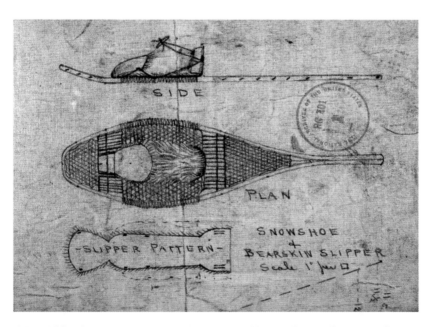

Figures 25 and 26   Snowshoes by Mellie Dunham and Robert Peary's Snowshoe Sketch. Peary worked with Maine snowshoe maker Mellie Dunham to create snowshoes to Peary's specifications. Native people in the treeless Arctic did not use snowshoes, but Peary's experience in Maine had taught him how useful they could be. He relied on them for traveling in soft snow and for crossing the thin ice of newly frozen leads or cracks in the ice.

through. The lead reopened just as they reached firm ice. They were now running short of food for men and dogs alike, killing the most exhausted dogs to feed both groups. But shortly after crossing "The Styx," they could see the mountainous coast of northern Greenland and in a few days were back on land and managed to catch some hares.

The storm that had first reopened the Big Lead had left the other teams at various places along the trail. Faced with drifting ice, and in some cases with only a compass to navigate, some lost their way. Bartlett, Wolf, and their teams continued to ferry supplies from Cape Hecla out to the sea ice in the hope that Peary's teams would find them on their way back. Marvin also continued on the trail, but he sent Ryan back to land to hunt so there would be fresh meat at Cape Hecla for the returning parties. With only a compass to navigate, Ryan's teams drifted and came to land some 50 miles west of where they intended, but they recognized their error and eventually made it back to the ship. Marvin also sent Clark and his teams back. Like Ryan's teams, they drifted, but east, not west. Misunderstanding their location, they headed southeast, expecting to reach Cape Hecla but instead ending up off northern Greenland. Marvin came across their trail and realized what had happened. Knowing they were short of food, he followed to try to catch them, but after a few days, with his own teams very short of provisions, he was forced to turn back. He arrived at the *Roosevelt* on May 21, and a fresh team was sent out to search for Clark. Meanwhile, Peary, Henson, and their teams had found Clark and the three Inughuit men on the Greenland coast, having seen their sledge tracks heading east, away from the ship and safety. They were nearly starving, having eaten all their dogs, as well as the hide lashings and even some of their mittens. Clark was in fear of his life, believing the Inughuit men were planning to kill him. How legitimate this fear was is open to discussion. Neither Clark nor the Inughuit men were fluent in each other's language, so there was plenty of room for misunderstanding on both sides, magnified by their terrible and frightening circumstances.

Finally, by June 3, everyone was back on board the ship. Peary spent the next two months or so sledging north and west, around the tip of Ellesmere Island (then called Grant Land), over to Axel Heiberg Island, where, from Cape Thomas Hubbard, he spotted "the snow-clad summits of the distant land in the northwest, above the ice horizon," later to be christened Crocker Land.

Figure 27   Peary Cairn at Cape Thomas Hubbard. The land Peary claimed to have seen from Cape Thomas Hubbard, which he named Crocker Land after one of his backers, turned out to be a mirage. Donald MacMillan confirmed this during an expedition from 1913 to 1917. This photograph was taken in the spring of 1914, when MacMillan had returned from a difficult journey out on the sea ice, during which no land was found.

While he was away, the *Roosevelt* broke free of the ice at Cape Sheridan and in early July was seven miles south at Cape Union. As Wardwell remarked in his journal, once the fast ice that had protected the ship had broken up, there was considerable danger for the ship: "We thought it best to get away from Cape Sheridan as we were in a position to get the pressure from the whole Arctic Ocean and don't know as we are much better off here, but think if we could get down a little further would be better off still, but I think the whole coast is bad and about the only safe place is out in the middle of the small ice and let the ship drift down with it." Peary and some of the Inughuit hunters were still away from the ship, however, so Bartlett dared not go too far.

On July 7, Wardwell's fears were realized when ice smashed the rudder, broke two blades off the propeller, and opened up a number of leaks. Over the following days the *Roosevelt* was pounded by the ice again and again. Miraculously, the vessel survived, although the damage was

Figure 28   Lowering the New Rudder.
On July 7 disaster struck. Wardwell wrote, "At 4 o'clock this morning the ice came in and smashed the rudder, broke two blades off the propeller, and the bean pot [cap] on the end of the shaft. It split things up in general and twisted things so can't start the engine. It takes 3 pumps to keep her free of water, have put all the provisions onshore clothing tents skins etc." For the next 18 days Bartlett, Wardwell, and the crew worked to remove the old rudder and construct a new one from scavenged ship parts. On July 28, they were finally able to lower it into place, where it worked reasonably well for a little while.

significant. Bartlett, Wardwell, and the crew spent the next few weeks working to repair the rudder, but they were only partially successful. While Peary had an extra propeller blade, he had not brought a spare rudder. After much effort, the remains of the damaged rudder were blasted off and a new rudder, fashioned from parts of the ship, was lowered into place.

Peary and the remaining Inughuit were all back on board in early August, and the *Roosevelt* began making its way south. Although it was only a distance of 330 miles, they did not reach Etah until the middle of September, spending days at a time locked in what the Inughuit later told Peary was unusually heavy ice. At Etah, Bartlett beached the ship so that they could examine the damage and perhaps improve on their repairs, with limited success.

The team's trip home was long and arduous. The new rudder performed poorly. In an address to the Explorers Club, Bartlett commented that the

Figure 29 *Roosevelt* **Beached to Repair Damage.** At Etah, Bartlett maneuvered the *Roosevelt* onto a beach at high tide, so that at low tide they could examine and perhaps repair the damaged rudder and propeller. They managed to do some work but were not able to make either of the damaged parts fully functional.

vessel now had a mind of its own and he had to use the sails to control the ship and move it south during favorable tides. In his journal, Wardwell describes efforts to deal with faulty boilers, a rudder and propeller repeatedly damaged by ice, and a dizzying array of mechanical problems. At critical times he had to shut down the boilers for days in order to rebuild valves. Without power, his men had to pump the badly leaking vessel by hand. Above deck, Bartlett was dealing with the failure of the steering mechanism. As if these problems were not enough, the vessel was short of fuel. Wardwell began to wonder whether the *Roosevelt* would be able to proceed south at all. In mid-October, the *Roosevelt* reached the coast of

Figure 30 Fresh Wood on Deck. Piles of freshly cut spruce trees, collected from the village of Hebron, in northern Labrador, are piled on the deck of the *Roosevelt*. The green wood was a poor substitute for coal, but they were low on fuel. The fresh wood did not burn well and Wardwell's firemen tried to help it along with anything they could find, including cod liver oil.

Labrador and limped south, its boilers burning green spruce, cod liver oil, blubber, and finally parts of the vessel.

Although the ship stopped in many communities along the coast, none had much coal to spare for them. In southern Labrador, fierce October storms delayed the ship's progress, and it was not until the end of November that they reached Sydney, Nova Scotia. There they could finally get coal but were unable to repair the rudder. They steamed on to New York in early December, still battling a failing engine and almost nonexistent steering. Finally, on Christmas Eve, six months after departing from Cape Sheridan, the *Roosevelt* docked in New York City, but not before (due to its compromised steering) the ship collided with the Wall Street ferry. That small disaster aside, the team members were welcomed home. "Every bell and whistle is going as we come along," wrote Wardwell.

Another Try: 1908–1909

Disappointed but undaunted, Peary began planning another expedition to the Pole before he even arrived home. On board the *Roosevelt* in 1906, he was already hatching plans for improvements to the vessel and fine-tuning his equipment and his approach. He was anxious to depart the very next summer, but between the repairs the *Roosevelt* needed and the alterations he had planned, the vessel would not be ready in time, so the departure was set for the summer of 1908.

Many elements of Peary's plan remained the same. He felt that in principle his method was sound, and had ice and weather conditions been better, he would have succeeded in 1906. As he had prophetically written in 1885, "Believe me there will come that season when the fortunate man waiting on the verge of the unknown region can speed away to the Pole." So 1906 had not been that season, but perhaps 1909 would be.

One change Peary made was to enlarge his team. Rather than rely on *Roosevelt* crewmen to lead some of the teams, he assembled a group of carefully chosen young men—the "scientific staff"—who would make the trip onto the sea ice and conduct research, particularly gathering tidal data. Among the experienced men, Matthew Henson was the most important. Robert A. Bartlett remained as captain of the *Roosevelt* and a key member of the sledging teams, and Ross Marvin also returned. George Borup, a young graduate of Yale University; Dr. John W. Goodsell, a physician and surgeon; and Donald B. MacMillan, a graduate of Peary's alma mater, Bowdoin College, were new to Arctic work, but all proved their mettle in the field. The ship's crew was made up of men from Bartlett's hometown of Brigus, Newfoundland, with the exception of George Wardwell, who, despite the difficulties of the last expedition, was willing to make the trip again.

The 1908 journey north was largely uneventful. They made good time to northern Greenland, where they once again hired Inughuit families, traded for dogs, hunted walrus for provisions, transferred coal from the *Erik*, and otherwise prepared themselves. Peary left supplies for the voyage home here and assigned two men to spend the winter at Etah, watching over them. The men, who took up residence in a house Frederick Cook had built at Anoritok, were also to look after supplies Cook had left at Etah and at Anoritok. Cook had arrived in Greenland the year before and set out for the North Pole. He had not yet arrived back in Greenland, however, so no one knew whether he had been successful. The man he had left to look after his supplies was not well and was eager to go home and sailed south on the *Erik*. Also staying behind in Greenland was Harry Whitney, a big-game hunter who had paid to sail north for summer hunting. However, upon learning that muskox hunting would not happen until the spring, he decided to stay for the winter.

Finally, on August 19, Peary and Bartlett were forcing their way through the pack ice in Kane Basin. They had hoped to take the ship farther north than in 1905, and Bartlett did manage to sail the *Roosevelt* a bit farther, setting a new record, but he found no good anchorage there. They returned to the familiar shores of Floeberg Beach, arriving on September 5, three years to the day from their first arrival. Once there, everyone quickly set to work.

As in 1905, some of the experienced members of the team set off on hunting trips, Inughuit women worked on sewing clothing for the expedition men, and the "tenderfeet" began to learn new skills. Less than two weeks after they arrived, Peary was already sending out sledges loaded with supplies north to Cape Columbia, where they would establish their last land base for the trip to the Pole, as well as parties to hunt and, in MacMillan's case, to map and survey. These early sledging journeys served multiple purposes. Setting up caches of supplies was a big job and essential to the success of the expedition, but the journeys were also early training for Borup, MacMillan, and Goodsell, in addition to ensuring that everyone was busy and in good physical condition after the enforced idleness of the trip north.

As their skills increased, Peary sent the men on longer trips. He had agreed to take tidal readings at various locations for the Coast and

Figure 31   A Fall Hunting Trip. Inughuit and American men hunted for caribou and muskox, as well as Arctic hare. The meat was important for feeding all the members of the expedition, as well as the dogs. The skins were used for clothing and bedding. All the hunting had a significant impact on local wildlife. In 1908, the men out hunting had to travel farther than in 1905, as the local animal populations had not recovered from the intensive hunting of the previous expedition.

Figure 32   Surveying and Mapping. Peary and his team used this theodolite to measure angles to determine the distance and altitude of landmarks so they could create detailed maps of poorly known coastlines and accurately record the location of tidal gauges. Peary had this instrument customized for work in cold conditions, even covering the small metal knobs with leather to protect his hands from the cold metal when he made fine adjustments.

Geodetic Survey (a precursor to the National Oceanic and Atmospheric Administration, or NOAA). In November, Peary sent MacMillan and Jack Barnes, one of the sailors, to Cape Columbia to establish a tidal gauge to be read once an hour for a lunar month. Two Inughuit men, Iggianguaq and Inukittoq, stayed with them, the men hunting as much as possible. In the cold and darkness, but living in a comfortable snow house, MacMillan and Barnes worked alternating six-hour shifts, gathering data, but learning as well. By the end of the month MacMillan wrote, "I hated to leave our snow Igloo. . . . We had thoroughly enjoyed associating with these people, now our friends, and had learned much . . . I had gained a new perspective." They had learned a great deal about Inughuit language and culture, and they had established the basis for good working relationships, and even lasting friendships. But they had also proven to Peary, and to themselves, that, properly supplied, they could survive for an extended journey, even in the darkness of the Arctic night.

LIGHT AND DARK

One often hears of the horrors of "six months of darkness" in the Arctic, but in fact the sun is below the horizon for six months only at the North Pole itself. Everywhere south of that the Arctic night is a bit shorter, until one reaches the Arctic Circle, where the sun does not rise only on the winter solstice. At Cape Sheridan, the sun sets for the winter in the middle of October and rises again at the beginning of March. But sunset does not mean immediate darkness. In the Far North the sun is always low in the sky, so there are very long periods of twilight. Weeks after the sun has set for the last time, and before it rises again in spring, there is a part of the day when there is some light in the sky. During the winter months moonlight is also important. When the moon is full in the Far North, it does not set, so as long as the sky is clear, moonlight reflected on snow and ice can provide great visibility for a part of every month.

MacMillan and Barnes arrived back at the ship in mid-December, and there was a brief lull in activity to celebrate Christmas. Immediately after, however, work resumed—the trip to the Pole would begin in only six weeks, and there was much to be done. After his experiences in 1906, Peary wanted to get an earlier start, so in mid-February, before the sun was up, the first sledging parties left the *Roosevelt* for Cape Columbia. By February 25, according to MacMillan, "The great white hills must have wondered what it was all about to see twenty-six men and one hundred and fifty dogs passing and repassing." Teams were ferrying supplies from caches established all along the 90-mile route from Cape Sheridan to Cape Columbia so that everything would be in place for the trip onto the sea ice. On February 28, the first teams left land to break trail. The next day the other teams followed. It was bitterly cold and the sun was not yet above the horizon, but ice conditions were much better than they had been in 1906. Unlike that year, they could see no open water and had high hopes that these conditions would continue.

So began many weeks of hard work, forcing sledges over pressure ridges, through drifted snow, and across leads of open water. Teams moved back and forth along the trail, some returning to Cape Columbia at intervals to pick up more supplies. When they had time, and if the ice was thin, they took soundings to gauge the depth of the ocean in order to identify the edge of the continental shelf. Often the ice was too thick, however, and the sounding line eventually broke, ending this effort.

Figure 33   Good Sledging. When the teams encountered stable and smooth ice, they could travel great distances with ease. The men sometimes sat on the sledges, but also walked or jogged alongside them. Such times were all too rare, unfortunately, and more often they struggled to maneuver the sledges across leads and through jumbled pressure ridges.

Their hopes for good ice conditions were soon dashed—in the first few days they crossed many leads, and on March 4 all forward progress was stopped for six days by the same "Big Lead" that had caused so much trouble in 1906. These were a very tense few days. Peary was concerned not only about the delay but also about supplies. Marvin and Borup were bringing much-needed fuel, but there was no word from them, and Peary had to decide whether to continue waiting if the lead closed or to move on and hope that they would eventually catch up. MacMillan eased some of the tension among the Inughuit by organizing races and other games with extravagant prizes. Eventually the lead closed, and although Marvin and Borup had not arrived, they moved on.

A few days later, the much-needed supplies arrived. By then the team had crossed numerous leads, and the strenuous work was taking its toll. On March 14, Goodsell, suffering from exhaustion made worse (as he thought) from formaldehyde in the pemmican, headed back to the ship, taking Uisaakkassak and Equ (both injured) back with him. The next day, MacMillan headed back as well, with severe frostbite in his heels. Peary regretted this development, writing, "It was a disappointment to me to lose MacMillan so early, as I had hoped that he would be able to go

Figure 34   Fun and Games on the Polar Sea. When a wide crack in the ice, or lead, halted progress toward the Pole, tension began to build among the team members. As a distraction, MacMillan organized a series of physical games with fantastic prizes. As Henson reported, "Most of the prizes are back on the ship and include the anchors, rudders, keel, and spars."

to a comparatively high latitude; but his disability did not affect the main proposition." All of the men knew that they were part of the supporting party and could be sent back at any time as fewer sledges were required to move supplies.

Borup was the next to return home, on March 20, followed by Marvin on March 27. That left Peary, Henson, Bartlett, and six Inughuit men. They were at 86°38' North, 232 miles from the Pole. On the first of April, at 87°48' North, it was Bartlett's turn to head south. The morning before he left, he walked five miles north, hoping to establish his own "furthest north" at 88°, but the drift of the ice foiled his attempt. "It was a tough blow to my pride," he wrote, "but made no real difference."

Peary, Henson, Odaq, Sigluk, Iggianguaq, and Ukkaujaaq were now 150 miles from the North Pole. They hoped to get there in five days, sledging 25 miles each day. This was the final dash, and their goal was to get there, and then safely back to land, as quickly as possible. Over the subsequent days they sledged ten hours at a time, sleeping only a few hours before setting off again. Early on April 5, they were 35 miles from the Pole. After

Figure 35 Sigluk, Odaq, Iggianguaq, and Ukkaujaaq. These four men, photographed by Matthew Henson after their return from the Pole, were among the best hunters and dog-sledge drivers in their community. Without their skills and courage, Peary could not have done his work.

12 hours of sledging, they were five miles away and stopped to rest. By noon on April 6, they had sledged the remaining distance. Henson, Odaq, and Ukkaujaaq had been breaking trail, with Henson leading. He stopped when he felt they had traveled five miles and waited for Peary and his team to catch up. Once he arrived and they had set up camp, Peary took a sextant reading, indicating that they were at 89°57' North.

They slept for a while, and then Peary set out again, heading north, to travel about ten miles before taking another reading. He returned to camp, took another reading (indicating that they had drifted a little west), and set off again, essentially crisscrossing the area and taking a number of readings in and around the Pole. He was aware that the ice was moving under him, and also knew that his instruments were not accurate enough to tell him when he was exactly at the Pole (unlike a modern GPS), so that he might be off by anywhere from one to five miles. These various short journeys were meant to ensure that at some point he was as close to the Pole as possible.

Figure 36   Peary's Camp at the North Pole. The North Pole is the imaginary point marking the northern end of the earth's axis. It is located on a sea of constantly shifting ice and so cannot be marked permanently, nor are there any landmarks to identify its location. As Peary wrote, "Precisely speaking, the North Pole is simply a mathematical point, and therefore, in accordance with the mathematical definition of a point it has neither length, breadth, nor thickness."

POLAR NAVIGATION

Finding one's way across a vast field of drifting sea ice is challenging. Once out of sight of land, there are no landmarks to follow, and depending on the drift of the ice you can be moving in any direction. Most of the teams had a compass, which worked well as long as they adjusted for the declination—they were many hundreds of miles north of the Magnetic North Pole to which the needle pointed. A compass can tell you what direction you are going, but to know where you are, you need more sophisticated equipment.

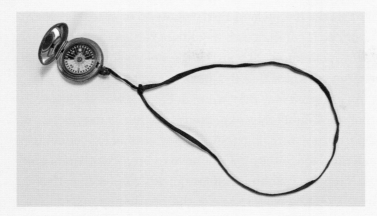

Figure 37   Peary's Pocket Compass.

Figure 38   MacMillan's 24-hour Watch.   Figure 39   Peary's Wool Undershirt with Pockets.

Peary and the men who were trained in navigation (including Marvin and Bartlett) used a sextant. By measuring the angle of the sun at its highest point to the horizon, they could calculate their latitude. They did not calculate their longitudes because they were so close to the Pole, where the lines converge, making it difficult to get an accurate determination. And, in any case, Peary believed such a determination would not be particularly useful. The men took 24-hour watches since they could not rely on light and dark to differentiate day and night. Peary carried his watch in a small pocket that Josephine sewed onto his woolen long underwear. By keeping the watch close to his body, he ensured that it did not freeze and kept accurate time.

Arriving at the Pole was the pinnacle of Peary's career, or at least it was meant to be, but it would be meaningless if he did not return to report his success. In all, the team spent about 30 hours at the Pole before the men set their sights on home. They all knew that the journey back to land could be the most dangerous. As it turned out, they were, in Peary's words, "agreeably disappointed" that the trouble they expected with the ice did not materialize. For the most part, they were able to follow the trail back, reducing their workload considerably since they did not have to break trail and could reuse their old igloos. Intent on reaching land as quickly as possible, they often "double marched," sledging back to one of their earlier igloos, stopping for a brief meal, and then continuing on to the next before sleeping. On a few occasions they managed a triple march. The sun was now so strong that they often traveled at night to avoid the worst glare in the middle of the day. They arrived back at Cape Columbia early in the morning of April 23 and spent two days there, sleeping, eating, and drying their clothes before heading back to the *Roosevelt*, where they arrived on April 27.

Peary's arrival back at the ship should have been a joyous occasion, but his success was clouded by a more immediate tragedy: Ross Marvin had died. According to the Inughuit men with whom he was traveling, Kudluktoq and Inukittoq (sometimes called "Harrigan" by the Americans, and also known as Inukitsuapaluk), Marvin had fallen through the young ice while crossing a lead, and they were unable to reach him. It was the type of tragic accident that was in all of their minds every time they crossed a lead. Many years later, Kudluktoq confessed that he had shot Marvin, as he feared Marvin's increasingly erratic and dangerous behavior would lead to Inukittoq's death. MacMillan steadfastly refused to believe this version of events. It is easy, however, to see how this could happen, as it had almost happened with Clark in 1906. The extreme physical and mental stresses all of the men were working under, combined with linguistic and cultural differences, could certainly have led to such a tragedy. Peary took Marvin's death very hard, as did the rest of the crew. They built a memorial to him on the top of Cape Sheridan and erected a cross with a metal plaque, made by Wardwell.

Peary did not expect the men who had returned to the ship before him to be idle. He had left instructions for work to be carried out in his absence, from laying in caches of food to taking more tidal readings. MacMillan and Borup left the ship in mid-April with five Inughuit men, heading for Cape Morris Jesup, the northernmost point of Greenland,

Figures 40–42   Ross Marvin and Memorial Tablet. Ross Marvin was Peary's senior assistant, responsible for the scientific aspects of the expedition, as well as being an important member of the sledging party. He was the only person to lose his life on these expeditions, and all the men felt the loss. Peary describes his reaction when he learned of Marvin's death: "The news staggered me, killing all the joy I had felt at the sight of the ship and her captain. It was indeed a bitter flavor in the cup of our success." Peary later wrote, "The bones of Ross G. Marvin lie farther north than those of any other human being. On the Northern shore of Grant Land we erected a cairn of stones and upon its summit we placed a rude tablet inscribed: 'In Memory of Ross G. Marvin of Cornell University, Aged 34. Drowned April 10, 1909 forty-five miles north of C. Columbia, returning from 86°38' N. Lat.'"

where they were to establish a camp for a series of tidal readings. On their way there, a journey of more than 300 miles, they passed the cairns marking the farthest north records of James Lockwood and David Brainard in 1882 and Peary in 1900. They took soundings northward from the cape and carefully monitored the tidal gauge for ten days, although the tide rose and fell only .38 feet (approximately 4.5 inches).

The *Roosevelt* broke free of the ice in early July, but it was a month before Bartlett could get the team to Greenland, where they spent nine days hunting walrus as a winter food supply for the Inughuit who had worked for them during peak hunting season. At Etah they got a hint of the trouble that was to come. In their absence, Cook had reappeared. He has spent the winter of 1908–1909 with his two Inughuit companions at Cape Sparbo on Devon Island, and they had only returned to Greenland in the spring of 1909. As Whitney reported to Peary, Cook immediately headed south to catch a Danish steamer to Copenhagen and then to the United States, leaving Whitney in charge of some of his equipment and papers. The two young men who had traveled with Cook—Ittukusuk and Aapilaq—were at Etah and were happy to tell anyone about their experiences. Matthew Henson in particular, the most fluent American Inuktitut speaker, interviewed them separately and also spoke with Panikpak, Ittukusuk's father, who went on part of the trip. The men each told the same story, emphasizing that they had gone out on the sea ice from Cape Thomas Hubbard but had never been out of sight of land. They repeated this story many times, to many different people over the years. Nevertheless, Peary's men learned from the crew of a ship that Cook claimed to have been to the Pole.

They sailed south in late August and in early September reached the first wireless stations on the Labrador coast—first a relay station at Indian Harbour, and then the main station at Battle Harbour. Finally, Peary could send telegrams south to his family, expedition backers, and the press, announcing "Stars and stripes nailed to the North pole." He stayed at Battle Harbour, waiting for the press and his family to arrive. There he gave his first press conference in the loft of the salt store. It would be many more months, however, before his success was officially acknowledged, and the debate over his achievement continues to this day.

3

PEARY THE INNOVATOR

Background

On April 6, 1909, when Peary, Henson, Sigluk, Ukkaujaaq, Iggianguaq, and Odaq reached what they believed was the North Pole, their success was no accident. Rather, it resulted from Peary's meticulous planning and attention to detail, his willingness to reevaluate the techniques and technologies he and his crews employed, his creativity and belief that he could solve most problems, and his ability to pick participants who excelled at what he asked them to do.

To reach the North Pole, Peary had to figure out how to get a ship as far north as possible to cut down on the amount of sledging his teams would need to do. He had to decide what would serve as the expedition's base of operations and where to put it. He had to think about how to move supplies and men from that base to the best point of land from which to strike out onto the sea ice, and then onto and across the moving, uneven frozen surface of the Arctic Ocean. He also had to consider how he would keep both men and dogs in good physical shape on the way to the North Pole, as well as on the way back.

At first glance, Peary's North Pole accomplishment seems rather straightforward. Peary and his team reached Cape Sheridan, on the northeastern-most coast of Ellesmere Island. From there, teams sledged to Cape Columbia, on the edge of the Polar Sea, using rugged, 15-foot-long, dog-drawn sledges fashioned out of oak. They made the trip many times, ferrying supplies while the inexperienced men learned the skills they would need on the ice. As they moved back and forth, they created a trail laden with caches and dotted with igloos that served as sleeping shelters. At set intervals teams returned to the ship, reducing the number of people and dogs on the ice as they got farther north. Finally, only Peary's and Henson's teams were left on the ice, and it was Henson who broke trail. Peary's team followed as they closed in on 90° North. On April 6 they reached the Pole, and on April 7 they dashed south, concerned with traversing the frozen sea before it began to break up under the warming April sun. Exhausted, they reached Cape Columbia on April 23 and on April 27 were back at Cape Sheridan. The *Roosevelt* was able to escape its ice-laden anchorage in late July and sail to northwestern Greenland to drop off the Inughuit families that had worked for the expedition. From there, the vessel turned south, arriving home in September. Behind this seemingly straightforward sequence of events, however, were years of planning, failing, inventing, and tinkering on Peary's part. Nothing was too insignificant to deserve his attention.

Robert E. Peary's Early Exploration Years

From the beginning in 1885, when Peary set his sights on investigating Greenland's inland ice, he carefully studied reports written about Arctic exploration and environmental conditions, paying special attention to the equipment used by other explorers. Before setting foot in the Arctic, he

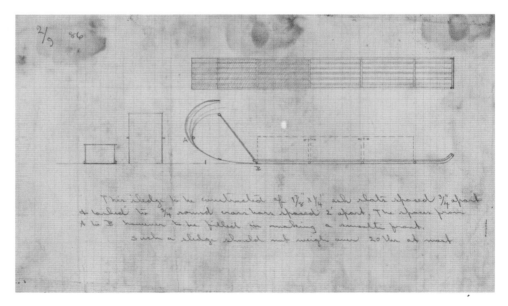

Figure 43　A Toboggan for the Inland Ice. The toboggans Peary used in 1886 were fashioned out of hickory, hide, and steel. Each was 9 feet long and 13 inches wide, with a turned-up bow to facilitate riding over snowdrifts. The toboggans were lightweight, each weighing 23 pounds, and could carry 200 pounds of gear, food, and fuel.

devised a plan to explore Greenland's inland ice using skis, snowshoes, and two bentwood toboggans that he designed.

Peary and his companion, Christian Maigaard, man-hauled the toboggans across the ice, and when wind and ice conditions were right they rode on them. The toboggans also served as windbreaks when the men stopped to eat or rest. Peary was sufficiently satisfied with the performance of the toboggans that at the end of the expedition he brought them back to the United States.

In 1890, Peary was trying to raise funds for another expedition to Greenland but was not particularly successful. During this discouraging time he was asked to give a lecture about his Greenland trip. It was well received, and he realized that lectures provided venues for him to raise money from audience members. Also, he noted that he could increase interest in his work by illustrating his lectures with photographs. He gathered up components of his Greenland outfit—fur clothes of Inuit design, skis, snowshoes, and a toboggan—and had a professional photographer take a series of studio photographs of him and his equipment. He had

Figure 44   Coasting. In his first book, *Northward Over the Great Ice,* Peary titled this photograph "Coasting," implying that it shows a relaxed way of descending a slope. This uncropped cyanotype print, probably a proof, makes it clear that the image was made in a studio rather than in the field. After his return from Greenland, Peary realized that illustrated lectures were an effective way to raise money, so he had studio photographs made to augment those taken on the actual trip.

some of the images hand tinted to increase their impact on his audiences and found them helpful when he was trying to raise interest in his work. Photography would be a component of all his future endeavors.

Peary was successful in interesting the Philadelphia Academy of Natural Sciences in his Greenland proposal, and in June 1891 the North Greenland Expedition set sail on the *Kite*. Expedition supplies included the toboggans from his earlier expedition and lumber to fashion new toboggans in Greenland. Skis and snowshoes continued to be important modes of transportation as well.

While arranging the expedition, Peary designed a house to serve as expedition headquarters and shipped the lumber with which to build it to Greenland. Red Cliff House, as the structure came to be called, was protected from the elements by an external wall that served as a wind break. Peary had planned on building this wall using local stone, expedition barrels, wooden crates, and turf. When ordering food and equipment,

Figure 45 Red Cliff House. The wall of barrels and crates around the house was roofed over with canvas and in winter insulated with snow. The crates were laid so that they were open to the inside of the corridor around the house, making it a convenient storeroom, easily accessible in all weather and saving space inside the house, as well as protecting it from the weather.

Peary had the construction of the wall in mind—he specified to suppliers that the crates in which the food and equipment were shipped had to be a certain height and width for ease of stacking. He would continue to use packing crates as construction materials throughout his career.

A Focus on Sledges

During the 1891–1892 expedition, Peary began working with local Inughuit, observing their technology and techniques of travel and food procurement. While the toboggans he had designed remained in use and he continued the man-hauling practice, increasingly he also included Inughuit and their dog-drawn sledges in his forays. The Inughuit's traditional short sledges were fashioned from whatever material was at hand—driftwood, antler, ivory, and bone. The sledges were built with upstanders at the back for steering and runners that angled up at the front. Later, Peary described in detail how Inughuit shoed their sledges with walrus hide and created extraordinarily smooth sledge shoe surfaces by applying warm urine and snow to the runners and letting them freeze.

That fall Peary began experimenting with sledge designs. He had new sledges constructed using his lumber supplies, and over the winter he personally built two sledges. At one point he had seven different sledge styles in use and kept notes on the performance of each, noting such things as what woods were used to make them, how they performed, and where they broke. For instance, a note dated 1891 details the characteristics and dimensions of Sledge No. 4, fashioned from pine. He recorded the sledge's overall length; various dimensions of its shoes, runners, and upstanders; the number of crossbars it had; how many separate pieces made up its shoes and runners; and its weight. Reflecting on his experience with dog-drawn sledges, he admitted that he had been wrong in believing that toboggans were superior to sledges.

By 1898, Peary had identified two characteristics that had to be considered when selecting or designing the equipment that would be carried on sledging expeditions. All equipment had to be lightweight, so the dogs could effectively pull fully loaded sledges. Equipment also had to be robust, able to endure use under difficult environmental conditions. He constantly balanced these two attributes—weight and durability—when designing and redesigning his equipment, including the sledges. He noted that the lighter the unloaded sledges, the more food could be carried on them. Sledges also needed to have strength so they could survive the

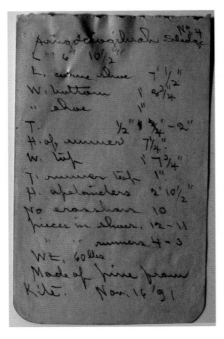

Figure 46 Early Sledges. In this note, Peary describes a sledge made in the fall of 1891 for or by an Inughuit man (possibly Ah-go-tok-suah in Lee's census of 1895), using pine supplied by Peary. He carefully recorded measurements for all the critical aspects of the sledge, from the length and height to the number of small pieces used to make the sled shoes.

bumps to which they were subjected on the inland ice when traveling over sastrugi (hard, parallel ridges of snow created by wind). Peary spent years trying to find the right balance of sledge weight and durability and load capacity.

In 1892, he returned to the United States a well-known Arctic explorer and immediately mounted another expedition to northwestern Greenland. Peary had observed that the indigenous people of the region were navigating the terrain he wanted to explore and doing so in relative comfort. Whereas many earlier explorers had either avoided interacting with local populations or looked down on them, Peary realized that his expeditions would benefit from adopting some of their technology and travel techniques.

During his 1893–1895 expedition, he continued to use sledges with raised beds and light runners when on the inland ice, but he began experimenting with a sledge built on what he termed the "native pattern." It was short, with upstanders at the rear, and its bed of slats ran perpendicular rather than parallel to the sled runners. The slats were lashed to the runners, and at the front the runners angled up slightly. He drew one of those sledges on January 19, 1895.

He experimented with the width of runners and the performance of iron sledge shoes. He studied sledge traction as well, calculating the resistance

Figure 47   A Sledge for the Inland Ice. The sledges Peary was using on the inland ice were lightweight affairs. Small posts attached to narrow bentwood runners raised the bed of the sledge above the ground. The narrow slats of the sledge bed were evenly spaced and ran lengthwise, parallel to the runners. He built sledges of various sizes on this model. At one point, he noted with great frustration that his largest sledge continued to break due to the repeated jolts to which it was subjected when traversing sastrugi, and he chafed at the amount of time that was lost repairing it.

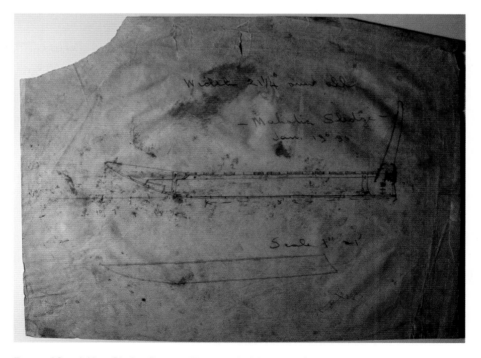

Figure 48   A New Sledge Design. This detailed drawing of a sledge, with every aspect of the sledge measured and carefully drawn to scale, demonstrates Peary's close attention to detail and his obsession with fine-tuning his equipment.

a sledge experienced on various kinds of terrain and surfaces. He also turned his attention to the dogs, carefully observing how much weight the average sledge dog could pull and how much each needed to eat in order to determine the ideal size of a dog team. Based on his experiences on this expedition, he completely converted to travel by dog-drawn sledges and extolled the virtues of northwestern Greenland dogs. Interestingly, Peary himself was not heavily involved in driving the dog-drawn sledges, though his assistant Matthew Henson was.

BURROS AND PASSENGER PIGEONS

In 1893, Peary took eight burros to Greenland to use as pack animals and quickly realized that this experiment was a mistake. The animals were ill suited to the region, and the sledge dogs were more than eager to eat them. He also tried using passenger pigeons as a means of communication between members of the expedition but soon abandoned that effort, as the birds suffered from the cold and fell prey to falcons and dogs. Reflecting on these failed experiments, he admitted that his excitement about the expedition had got the best of him, and he returned to his more methodical practice of careful experimentation and refinement of technologies.

As Peary shifted his focus from exploring the inland ice to exploring northwestern Greenland, and then to traversing the Arctic Ocean in an effort to reach the North Pole, he realized that the sledges used on the inland ice were inadequate for work along the shores and on the jumble of hard, rafted ice on portions of the Polar Sea. In his book, *The Secrets of Polar Travel*, he explains that he zeroed in on the essential characteristics of a sledge that could work such terrain, noting that it had to be able to carry a heavy load, a dog team had to be able to pull it, and a person had to be able to maneuver it. These considerations had to be balanced against a sledge's strength and capacity to withstand the twists and turns, crashes, and sideslips to which it would be subjected when pulled through mountain passes and over pressure ridges.

Peary's effort to reach the North Pole in 1905–1906 failed when a large lead impeded his journey and he exhausted his supply of food while waiting for the lead to close or ice over. He returned to the United States confident in his basic approach but admitted that he still needed to refine it, as well as components of the expedition outfit.

He was not satisfied with his sledges, so he took another close look at the traditional Inughuit sledge, which was three to four feet long and fashioned out of driftwood, ivory, bone, and antler. He noted that these components were all lashed together with sealskin or walrus hide; the sledge did not contain a single peg or nail. He realized that the Inughuit had designed the perfect sledge for the conditions and terrain his team had to navigate. The Inughuit sledge could withstand travel over hard, uneven ice because its parts were lashed together, giving the sledge great flexibility. A sledge's various components could twist and turn as it traveled across uneven ground and lumpy pressure ridges. He adopted the Inughuit design, increasing the size of the sledge, slightly altering its front and back ends, and building it out of expanses of oak and ash.

Figure 49   The Peary Sledge. An unidentified Inughuit man drives a Peary-style sledge while MacMillan watches. The sledge is lightly loaded with only two crates lashed down among some other equipment, but these long sledges could easily carry much more.

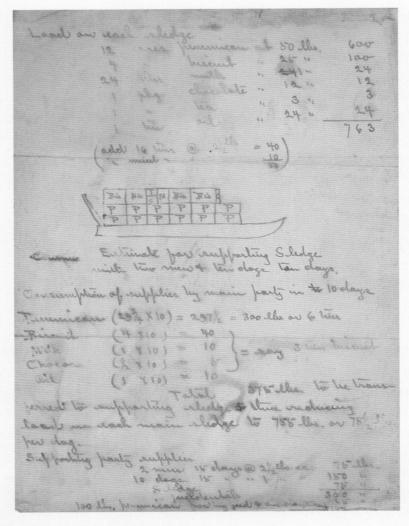

Figure 50   Peary's Calculations for Loading a Sledge.

LOADING A SLEDGE

Peary realized that he had to pay attention to the weight and volume of the load a sledge would carry so people could stay out for prolonged periods of time with enough food for dogs and humans while still allowing the men to handle the sledges and the dogs to pull them. He specified how sledges were to be loaded. Supplies were prepackaged in the United States to specific sizes and weights and coded according to a system he had devised. Each sledge was loaded keeping in mind that food (tea, condensed milk, and pemmican) and tools (utilitarian knife, large knife to cut snow blocks, and ax to chop a trail through pressure ridges) needed to be immediately accessible, so they should be at the top of the load. He understood that expeditions could fail due to inattention to detail, and his men would also be more comfortable and work most efficiently if things were planned well.

Camp Stoves

In addition to modes of travel, throughout his career Peary was fascinated by the designs of camp stoves. He understood that nutrition and hydration were essential for working under difficult conditions. On land his teams hunted for food, but on the sea ice dogs and men needed to carry their food with them, in the form of pemmican (one type for dogs, another for humans). Water was also of considerable concern. When sledging parties stopped to rest, having a hot beverage ready was important, so carrying a stove that could turn ice into boiling water quickly was essential. Peary detailed the ideal parameters: cook stoves had to be as light as possible, use as little fuel as possible, and melt ice and boil water efficiently and quickly. Also, the lighter the cooking contraption and the less fuel it required, the more food could be carried on a sledge.

Before the 1908–1909 expedition got under way, MacMillan was summoned to Peary's New York City hotel room. In an account of the expedition, MacMillan describes entering the room and observing that the entire back of it was taken up with camp stoves that Peary had ordered and was testing. None of them satisfied all his criteria. Eventually, Peary designed, and Henson and Chief Engineer George Wardwell (assisted by firemen on the *Roosevelt*) constructed, lightweight stoves that burned alcohol. They held enough fuel (6 ounces) and burned hot enough to turn ice into boiling water in nine minutes and then went out. MacMillan wrote that when the men stopped for a break, they eagerly placed their sore, chapped hands around the stove, and he noted how disappointing it was when the stove went out, the fuel allotment, held in the stove's reservoir, having been expended. The stoves, carried on the sledges in metal boxes, worked well, except when temperatures were so low that the alcohol could not vaporize. The solution to this problem was to heat the alcohol by burning paper or cloth.

The Design and Redesign of a Vessel

Around 1903, the man who spent decades perfecting the designs of stoves and sledges took on a larger project: the design of a vessel that could penetrate the ice-laden straits separating Ellesmere Island and Greenland and withstand being frozen into the ice for nine months to a year. Arctic vessels at the time had strengthened hulls, but their captains knew it was best to avoid the ice as much as possible, since the rock-hard material could easily puncture the hull of a ship. Peary wanted a ship that was

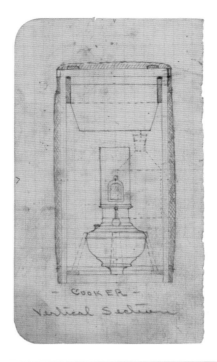

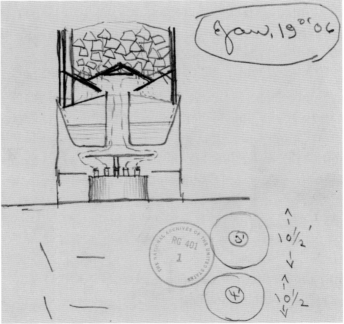

Figures 51 and 52 Stove Plans. Peary's papers and correspondence, housed at the National Archives and Records Administration, are filled with doodles of stoves, drawn in the margins of documents and drafts of letters, as well as formal drawings of the devices. For years he played with stove designs. The formal vertical section of a cooker is from early in his career and seems to be based on a traditional lamp with an elegant fluted fuel reservoir. A more informal sketch, made aboard the *Roosevelt* in the winter of 1906, includes both the stove design and a method for melting ice using steam from hot meltwater to accelerate the process.

nimble and robust and that, under steam power, was strong enough to push ice out of the way and even crush ice in its path. He derived some of his inspiration for the design of such a ship from Fridtjof Nansen's *Fram*, other ships that had plied Arctic and Antarctic waters, and his experience sailing on other Arctic vessels.

The SS *Roosevelt*, a 184-foot-long auxiliary steamship, designed by William Winant according to Peary's specifications, was that vessel. Built at the McKay and Dix Shipyard on Verona Island, near Bucksport, Maine, and outfitted with masts and boilers at the Portland Company in Portland, Maine, the *Roosevelt* had a heavily reinforced wooden hull that was 24–30 inches thick, made out of oak and yellow pine. Its powerful compound steam engine was designed to be powered by two Almy water-tube boilers and a powerful Scotch boiler, which collectively provided 1,000 horse-power. The Almy boilers also were to provide heat and power when the engine was not running—critical since the *Roosevelt* would be the base of operations throughout the fall, winter, and spring when frozen into the ice.

Peary anticipated that the ship's propeller would be at risk given the amount of ice through which the vessel would navigate, so the ship was equipped with replacement blades, and in theory the propeller system could be lifted through the hull should repairs be necessary. Also, he equipped the *Roosevelt* with sails to be used if the engines should fail or to assist in maneuvering the vessel. Concerned that the crew would be living on the ship for more than a year, Peary placed crew quarters above deck to maximize access to fresh air, and because there was no room below deck given the extensive bracing of the hull.

The *Roosevelt*'s bow had a sharp wedge shape and was solidly built, as it was designed to slice through ice that the ship did not push out of the way or crush. The propeller and rudder were tucked under the hull to mini-mize their exposure to ice, and the hull had a slight egg shape, so that the vessel would rise if squeezed between two pans of ice. The vessel also had a shallow draft so it could ply near-shore waters. Peary's plan was to get the *Roosevelt* as far north as possible, freeze the vessel into the ice, and use it as the base of operations for sledging relays over the ice.

The *Roosevelt*'s maiden voyage did not go smoothly. The vessel's Almy boilers were not reliable and constantly had to be rebuilt by George Wardwell and his firemen. Despite all of Wardwell's efforts, the boilers remained unpredictable. In addition, some of the ship's bracing was placed too close to the boilers, so during the first few weeks some of the

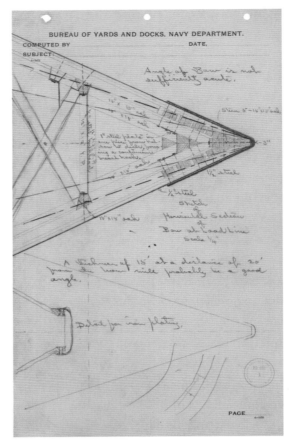

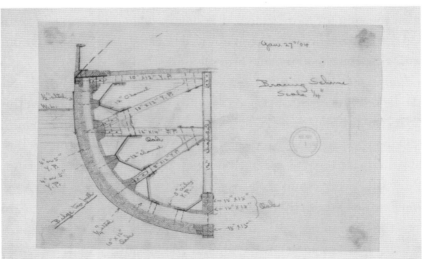

Figures 53 and 54   Heavy Bracing. Peary was actively involved in the design and construction of the *Roosevelt*. In this drawing of the bow of the ship, he notes that the angle of the bow is too wide and specifies the size and placement of thick oak boards and steel plates. The bracing section clearly shows the double oak planks on the hull and the heavy cross bracing that gave the ship its strength.

bracing caught fire and had to be cut away to avoid disaster. While the ship was making progress, one of the boilers was often down, so the vessel operated at half-speed.

The *Roosevelt* performed well otherwise. In fact, Peary and Bartlett were delighted with the way the ship handled, though they noted that it rolled due to its configuration and the fact that it carried such a heavy load on deck. Bartlett, with Peary's full support, rammed the vessel through ice, dodging heavy ice floes, and smashing through pack ice. Despite many close calls, the *Roosevelt* survived, though not unscathed. When they finally returned to New York in December 1906, after a very long and difficult voyage, people were shocked by the condition of the vessel. Peary understood what he needed to do to fix the *Roosevelt*'s problems and persuaded his backers to fund renovations, despite the appalling condition of the ship. A new propeller was installed, the rudder was replaced, the boilers were replaced, and crew quarters were improved.

Figure 55   The *Roosevelt* in Dry Dock. The *Roosevelt*'s propeller was tucked well under its stern to protect it from ice; despite this precaution, it was severely damaged in 1906. A new propeller was installed during the repairs and renovations to the vessel in 1907–1908, and on the 1908–1909 voyage it performed well, escaping any serious damage.

The *Roosevelt* had cost a little more than $100,000 to build, and the repairs ran to $75,000 and took a year longer to complete than Peary had hoped. But the ship would make the trip to Cape Sheridan and back without incident, performing exactly as Peary had planned.

On July 6, 1908, the *Roosevelt* left its berth in New York City, with George Wardwell and Robert Bartlett assuming their positions as chief engineer and captain. The trip north was uneventful, and despite efforts to get north of Cape Sheridan, the men found themselves back at their old anchorage. Supplies were offloaded, including crates of food, as a precaution in case the ship were to sink or catch fire. Peary had continued the practice of specifying the dimensions of the crates in which food and supplies were packed. The food crates were used to build "crate houses" that actually served as workshops. Henson and Inughuit men used one as a workshop in which to build sledges. The sledges were shoed with iron shoes manufactured by the chief engineer's crew, also involved in manufacturing camp stoves on shore. Remains of these workshops are evident at Cape Sheridan, where archaeologists have found tent rings and crate house outlines, coal from a crate house wood-burning stove, pieces

Figure 56   Crate Houses. As he had done since 1891, Peary specified the sizes of crates for food and equipment so that they could be used to construct shelters that served as workshops and, if necessary, refuges in the event of the ship being crushed or burned. The remains of three crate houses from 1908 to 1909 are still clearly visible on Floeberg Beach, where organic matter left behind has acted as fertilizer for a thick carpet of moss and other plants.

of sawed oak planks and sledge runners, pieces of crates bearing Peary's name and the names of manufacturers, food bones, and the remains of tin cans.

Work throughout the Year

Where previous explorers had spent the dark months trying to pass the time at headquarters, staging plays, reading, getting out of shape, and irritating one another, early in his career Peary recognized that travel during the Arctic winters was possible and desirable. In 1908–1909, everyone was put to work immediately. Westerners learned the art of driving dog teams, Inughuit women sewed and repaired fur clothing, people made sledges, and a weather observatory was maintained. Peary sent teams out to hunt, take tidal readings, and establish caches of food and supplies. Inughuit made trips to Lake Hazen to hunt and fish, and Westerners and Inughuit, who could not speak the same language, learned to work together.

In the spring, Borup and MacMillan (two greenhorns when it came to Arctic work) found themselves farther north than most seasoned explorers had been. Accounts written by those experienced explorers were peppered with reports of great suffering. By contrast, MacMillan, in his book about his experiences on the expedition, noted that, due to the training

Figure 57   The Cape Morris Jesup Grenadiers. Peary's methods worked so well that MacMillan and Borup, with a small group of Inughuit men, felt comfortable sledging more than 300 miles to Cape Morris Jesup, the northern extremity of Greenland, to conduct research. A good time seems to have been had by all. Here Borup has photographed the team with muskox furs on their heads and rifles, captioned by MacMillan "the Cape Morris Jesup Grenadiers."

he and Borup had received and Peary's system of travel, they had time to have fun; indeed, they were having "the time of their lives."

Relay System and Strategy

In 1909, once the days started getting longer (though temperatures were still in the –20° to –40°F range), Peary began deploying parties of men north to Cape Columbia, their sledges laden with supplies. The teams were tasked with traveling onto the sea ice, cutting a trail through jagged pressure ridges, leaving supplies of food and equipment at specific intervals, and returning to the *Roosevelt* for more supplies. As various sledge parties traversed the same route repeatedly, they created a somewhat groomed trail, though it was constantly shifting due to the movement of the sea ice, and the journeys over the sea ice were often perilous, as leads opened and closed, ice pans ground against one another, and equipment and sledges required repair.

Figure 58 Sledges Leaving the *Roosevelt*. There was constant traffic of sledges leaving from and arriving back at the *Roosevelt* as Peary sent men out to hunt, record tidal readings, and establish caches for the spring trip to the Pole. The early trips were often brief, as the untrained men learned the ropes, but soon they were away for days or even weeks at a time.

On February 22, 1909, Peary left the *Roosevelt* to join the other sledge parties at Cape Columbia. He continued to deploy sledging parties along the route to the Pole with instructions about where to establish supply caches or depots. Eventually he sent most of the sledging parties off on other assignments. Bartlett's party was the last to turn back on April 1, close to the 88th parallel.

The men Peary chose to be members of the North Pole party were Henson, who was an excellent dog-sledge driver, and four of the most talented Inughuit drivers and travelers. With them were forty of the strongest dogs, pulling five sledges. They traveled along the established route with relative ease, using supplies cached along the way and snow shelters built at various intervals. Eventually, they, too, had to break trail. Travel was not easy by any means, but Peary's system, honed through years of trial and error and analysis, ensured that it was as efficient and effective as possible. Peary reported that initially the team encountered pressure ridges and progress was slow. The men also encountered relatively smooth ice and sometimes made fantastic time. Everyone's skills were tested, however, as they contended with leads and strong winds, and there was no denying that the trip across moving ice was unnerving.

Public Relations

Peary and his wife Josephine were effective fundraisers who understood the importance of public relations. In addition to public and private lectures, often illustrated with lantern slide shows, Josephine wrote articles (as well as a children's book), was on the radio, and decorated their home with Arctic memorabilia. Peary adopted the practice of naming major landforms after his key benefactors and giving the donors Arctic-themed gifts. One such individual was Thomas Hamlin Hubbard, a fellow Bowdoin College graduate and an influential member of the New York business community who helped finance Peary's 1908–1909 North Pole expedition. He was also president of the Peary Arctic Club. Peary named a major cape on Axel Heiberg Island, a far northern island in what is now Nunavut, after Hubbard, and he named Cape Morris Jesup after one of his early New York benefactors.

HUBBARD SLEDGE

In 1910, Peary, a graduate of Bowdoin College in Brunswick, Maine, gave one of the sledges used to reach the North Pole to Thomas Hamlin Hubbard, a railroad executive and philanthropist (Bowdoin Class of 1857), in recognition of Hubbard's financial contributions to Peary's expeditions. Earlier, Peary had acknowledged his backer's support by naming a cape on Grant Land after him. Hubbard financed numerous building projects on the campus of his alma mater, including Hubbard Hall, built to house the college's library. Hubbard gave the sledge to the Bowdoin Alumni Club. In 1967, when the Peary-MacMillan Arctic Museum opened in Hubbard Hall, the Alumni Club transferred the sledge to the Arctic Museum. Today, the sledge sits in a climate-controlled case in the foyer of the building, a reminder of the college's northern links that extend back to 1860 and also testimony to Peary's inventiveness.

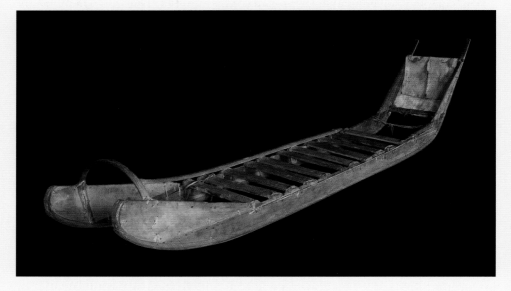

Figure 59   The Hubbard Sledge.

Peary had Henson make sledges of various sizes while the *Roosevelt* steamed south in 1909. The sledges were to be souvenir gifts to Peary's backers. Also, he brought back the five sledges that had been to the North Pole. These battered sledges would also become souvenir gifts. Peary gave Hubbard one of the sledges, which came to be known as the Hubbard Sledge, and Hubbard gave it to Bowdoin College.

Before becoming gifts, the battered North Pole sledges served one more purpose: They were part of the scene created by Peary on the deck of the

Figure 60   Press Photos. Journalists from the United States and Canada arrived in Battle Harbour to cover the breaking news story of Peary's return from the North Pole. The men donned their warm fur clothing and posed for photographs next to a souvenir sledge on the deck of the *Roosevelt*, little imagining the media frenzy that would soon develop.

Roosevelt for the benefit of dozens of reporters and photographers who rushed to Battle Harbour, Labrador, to be present at Peary's first press conference since reaching the Pole. Henson, MacMillan, Borup, and Goodsell (as well as Tom Gushue, the first mate), attired in fur clothing, posed sitting on or standing next to the sledges on the deck of the *Roosevelt*.

In all likelihood, people taking the photographs barely noticed the carefully designed sledges on the deck of the ingeniously built ship, as they were simply the stage. The fur-clad Westerners symbolized the exotic distant place Peary had dared to explore. However, today we can see the scene depicted in the photographs in a different light, for it contains many of the ingredients that contributed to Peary's success: the innovative ship, the sledge that drew inspiration from Inughuit designs, the fur clothes sewn by Inughuit women, and the well-fed men symbolize Peary's inventive side, his open-mindedness, and his confidence that he could solve most problems. He looked for solutions everywhere, be it in a machine shop or an Inughuit village. He invented and fine-tuned technology and techniques, surrounded himself with accomplished people whom he trained well and kept comfortable and relatively happy, and never missed an opportunity to learn from his mistakes.

4

HE COULD NOT DO WITHOUT THEM

Popular history has long focused on Peary as an individual, portraying him variously as a hero or a villain depending on the perspective of the writer, but, like most heroes (and villains), he did not achieve his fame alone. Indeed, one of his successes was his ability to identify people who shared his goals, ambitions, and dedication to the cause and to inspire in them a deep loyalty that carried them through difficult times. The list of all the people whose hard work and dedication helped advance Peary's career is too long to include here, and we will limit our focus to those who were the most important: his wife, Josephine; his long-time assistant, Matthew Henson; the captain of the SS *Roosevelt*, Robert Bartlett; and Peary's assistants on the 1908–1909 expedition. The Inughuit, in many ways the most important of all, are the subject of the next chapter.

Josephine Diebitsch Peary

From the day they married in 1888, Josephine was Peary's strongest and most loyal supporter. She stood by him through years of absence, infidelity, and stubborn devotion to a project that must at times have seemed as unobtainable as the moon. In her own way, however, she was just as adventurous and determined as he was. As a key contributor to his success, she kept their family going during his long trips north, overcame shyness to become a public speaker, published books to raise money for his work, approached donors to help fund and organize relief expeditions to bring him home, and herself traveled to the Arctic many times, both with and without him. All in all, she was a most unusual woman for her time.

Josephine's devotion to Peary, and her own adventurous spirit, lay behind her initial decision to accompany him to Greenland in 1891. She was the first American woman to venture so far north, and the fact that she would even consider such a journey is remarkable. She embraced the opportunity, however, and proved to be up to the challenge. She had always loved the outdoors and was no stranger to long hikes, or even hunting. She tackled life in the North head on. Although she was not part of the team sledging on the ice cap, she did go on hunting trips, learned to use snowshoes so she could go for a walk every day in all but the worst weather, and even devised a fur costume to wear that was more sensible than the long dresses she would have worn at home, while preserving her modesty.

While Josephine did not endure the difficulties of Peary's long trip across the ice cap, she did have some adventures of her own. Most memorable, perhaps, was a camping trip with Matthew Henson to the head of MacCormick Fjord, where they anticipated that Peary would descend from the ice cap in the summer of 1892. As they waited, they spent the days hiking, hunting, and enjoying nature. One day they decided to leave some treats at a cache they expected Peary to encounter on his way back.

Figure 61   At Home in the North. Josephine Peary took to heart her husband's conviction that it was possible to make a comfortable home in the Far North. While there, she made a point of going out in all but the very worst weather, regularly walking and snowshoeing. With Peary, she traveled in small boats and on dog sledges and camped, both out of necessity and for pleasure.

They hiked to the cache but were trapped when a glacial river they had crossed with some effort at low tide became impassable. Finally, 24 hours later, they were able to cross the river again and return to their camp. Josephine wrote, "We were perfectly numb with cold from mid-thigh down, and so ran and pounded our feet and limbs for the three miles that intervened between the river and the tent, which we reached in an hour. Thus far we feel no ill results from our icy adventure."

The challenges of that first year in the Arctic did not daunt Josephine, and in 1893 she was eager to return, despite being pregnant with her first child. She hired a nurse, Susan Cross, to accompany her and set off again. She safely delivered the baby—a daughter—on September 12, 1893. Marie Ahnighito Peary (also known as the "Snow Baby") enlivened life at Anniversary Lodge as she grew through her first year. True to form, once she was old enough and the sun had returned in mid-February, her mother ensured that Marie got outside every day, no matter how cold, often riding in a small dog-drawn sled. In the summer of 1894, Josephine reluctantly returned home with Marie, leaving Robert behind for another year. With her was Eqariusaq (called "Miss Bill" by Josephine, and "Billy Bah" by baby Marie), who was to spend the year with them in Philadelphia before returning on the ship that was to bring Peary home in 1895.

Figure 62 Marie Ahnighito Peary.
Peary described his daughter, Marie Ahnighito, as "a little blue-eyed snowflake, born at the close of the arctic summer day." She was called the "Snow Baby" by the Inughuit, because of her pale skin.

EQARIUSAQ

Eqariusaq was only 12 when she befriended Josephine and baby Marie in northern Greenland. It is impossible to know how she felt about accompanying them to their home in Philadelphia, but hopefully she was excited, even if she knew little about what to expect. She boarded the *Falcon* in her traditional clothing, but Josephine soon saw to it that she was outfitted with garments more appropriate for her destination and also cut her hair (presumably out of fear that she had head lice).

Figures 63 and 64   Eqariusaq on Board the *Falcon* in Her Own Clothing and a New Dress.

Once in the United States, Eqariusaq (or "Billy Bah," as Marie called her) was treated as part of the Peary family. She did not know enough English to attend school, so she stayed home, helping Josephine care for Marie. As Josephine and later Marie described, Eqariusaq learned a great deal while she was with them, including the fact that, unlike at home, while she was out walking she could not just leave things on the street and expect to find them still there when she went to retrieve them.

Figure 65   Eqariusaq with Marie.

"Miss Bill" returned home in 1894 on the ship that went to fetch Peary. She had grown out of her fur clothing, but someone (perhaps Josephine's brother Emil) purchased some western Greenland–style clothing for her at a stop on the way north. She was happily reunited with her family, full of stories of the strange things she had seen. Her tales may have seemed so outlandish that many did not believe them, and in later years she reportedly refused to talk about her experiences in the south. As an adult, she once again encountered Peary and worked as a seamstress on the 1908–1909 expedition.

Figure 66   Eqariusaq (left) Reunited with Her Family.

Figure 67   Eqariusaq on
Board the SS *Roosevelt*.

The Peary family returned to Greenland again in the summer of 1897 to retrieve a huge iron meteorite, and in the summer of 1900 Josephine made another trip north, bringing Marie along on what she anticipated would be a summer trip, hoping to convince Robert to come home. She carried with her the sad news that their second child, Francine, had died at the age of eight months, having never seen her father.

This trip would turn out to be the most challenging of the visits Josephine made. When their ship, the *Windward*, arrived in Smith Sound, they discovered that Peary was away, hundreds of miles north at Fort Conger on Ellesmere Island. To make matters worse, storms and drifting ice trapped them in Payer Harbour, forcing them to winter there. The final blow was Josephine's discovery of Peary's liaison with Aleqasina, who had recently borne him a son. Josephine was heartbroken and wrote to Peary expressing her feelings of love and despair, but also her conviction that he should not give up his work. To her credit, however, and despite her typically nineteenth-century views of Inughuit in general, she was not hostile toward Aleqasina. Rather, Josephine saw to it that Aleqasina was welcomed into her cabin on the *Windward* and even nursed her when she fell ill.

It was May 1901 when Peary finally learned that Josephine and Marie were there. How he and Josephine came to terms with their situation is unknown, but somehow Josephine found a way to forgive him, and she remained devoted to him for the rest of her life. She and Marie returned home again that summer, and in 1902 Josephine made one final trip north. The following spring, their son, Robert Jr., was born, and although both he and Marie would travel north as adults, Josephine never returned to the Arctic.

As remarkable and important as Josephine's trips to the North were, it was her work at home while Peary was in the field that contributed most to his career. Arctic exploration was a very expensive undertaking, and the Pearys were by no means wealthy. Funding from private donors was essential, and the exigencies of work in the Arctic often meant that unanticipated expenses arose. In 1894, when Josephine and Marie returned home, the plan had been that Peary and the rest of the team would return as well. But when Peary decided to stay in the North for another year, it meant that he would need to find another way to get home. It fell to Josephine to find the money, and the ship, to bring him and his team back to the United States.

Luckily, although she probably would have denied it, Josephine was better prepared for this new direction in her life than most women of her time. As an 1890 graduate of the Spencerian Business College (one of only six women in her class), and having worked for both the Department of the Interior and the Smithsonian Institution before her marriage, she was well versed in managing money and other business practices. As anthropologist and historian Patricia Erikson put it, she was "a smart, well-educated, multilingual, well-placed member of intellectual and bureaucratic circles in the nation's capital." While she had no experience in fundraising, she was well aware of how her husband approached this aspect of his work, and when the necessity arose, she found herself equal to the task.

In 1893, Josephine had already published one book, an account of her experiences in 1891–1892. In 1894, she began writing letters to individuals and societies soliciting funds to hire a vessel to retrieve her husband, which generated some of the $10,000 required, but it was not enough. She approached Morris K. Jesup, the wealthy philanthropist and president of the American Museum of Natural History, and although, as she later described, "all the courage oozed out of her shoes" as she prepared to enter his office, he found her request compelling and assured her that he would make sure that the ship would sail in the spring. Jesup went on to become one of Peary's greatest supporters. Josephine even agreed to give public lectures, including one for the National Geographic Society, raising an additional $2,000.

This first taste of fundraising was far from the last. Josephine would go on to publish two more books to help fund her husband's work, in addition to managing his correspondence and all the other organizational details that required attention while he was away. She was often in the public eye as well, granting numerous interviews and ensuring that Peary's name and goal were not forgotten during his long absences. Erikson has shown how Josephine managed some aspects of this process, including the carefully decorated parlor in which she was sometimes photographed wearing elegant clothing and surrounded by furs, tusks, harpoons, and other reminders of the adventures she had shared with her husband.

Her adventurous spirit notwithstanding, Josephine was still a woman of her time. As bold as she was, she insisted that everything she did, from traveling to the Arctic to lecturing and granting press interviews, was in support of her husband's work, and that her first duty was to him. She was, of course, also "The Mother of the Snow Baby," a title that followed her for

Figure 68 Josephine at Home. Historian Patricia Erikson has described how Josephine "domesticated" her northern homes and contrasted that with how she brought the distant, exotic Arctic into her American home. Here her elegant and fashionable dress contrasts with the many animal furs and tusks she has artfully arranged in the sitting room of the Pearys' apartment. Beside her is a silver teapot and cups for her and her guest. These may be her "penny cups," fine china tea cups she had saved her pennies to purchase, emblematic of her good taste, but also of the economies she had to practice at home in order to support her husband's work.

the rest of her life. Josephine retired from the public eye after her husband's death but lived a long life enriched by her children and grandchildren. She died in 1955 and is buried alongside Robert in Arlington National Cemetery.

Matthew Alexander Henson

Matthew Henson first went north with Peary in 1891. He was with him on his long trip over the Greenland Ice Cap in 1893. He was with him when he rounded the northern end of Greenland in 1900. He was with him off Cape Hecla in 1902. He was with him in 1906 when he broke the world's record. He was the most popular man aboard the ship with the Eskimos. He could talk their language like a native. He made all the sledges which went to the Pole. He made all the stoves. Henson, the colored man, went to the Pole with Peary because he was a better man than any of his white assistants. As Peary himself admitted, "I can't get along without Henson."

—Donald B. MacMillan, 1934

Of all the people Peary relied on, Matthew Henson is perhaps the most remarkable. Born to a free black family in Maryland just one year after the end of the Civil War, Henson would seem to have been an unlikely candidate for Arctic exploration. Yet he thrived in the North, becoming a skilled hunter and dog-sledge driver who was fluent in the Inughuit language. The Inughuit accepted him as a member of the community in ways that Peary never was, nor sought to be. Peary would not have succeeded without Henson, and he was well aware of that fact. But neither Peary nor American society in general were willing to give Henson the accolades he deserved when they returned from the Arctic for the last time in 1909. While all the white members of the team were included in public ceremonies, awarded medals, and otherwise celebrated, Henson was not. Despite having been the only other American to have stood at the North Pole with Peary, once back home he was seen as merely a servant, relegated to the background and largely excluded from the

Figure 69   Matthew Henson. Everyone who worked with Henson was struck by his many talents, good nature, and courage. The skills he learned from the Inughuit, from managing dog teams to speaking their language, made him indispensable to Peary. Here he stands among a group of Inughuit men and boys, with two women (in their tall sealskin boots) behind them. Like the Inughuit men, Henson is wearing polar bear skin pants and sealskin boots, but in this summer photograph he wears his cloth coat and cap instead of warmer gear.

honors granted to the others. Only with the dawn of the civil rights era did he begin to receive his due.

Thanks in part to increased interest in Henson toward the end of his life, his basic biographical details are well known. Born in 1866, he went to sea at the age of 12 and was fortunate in working for Captain Childs, who recognized his capacity for learning and saw to it that he continued his education while on board ship. He traveled the world for ten years, but by 1888 he was back in Baltimore. There he worked for a haberdasher, who, like Childs, must have seen something in him, for when Peary came in to purchase equipment for his second trip to Nicaragua and mentioned that he was also looking for a manservant, the proprietor recommended Henson.

Henson traveled to Nicaragua as Peary's valet but once there proved himself so useful that he was soon promoted to a member of the survey team. He continued to work for Peary as a messenger when they returned to Washington, D.C., in 1890 and agreed to accompany him to Greenland in 1891. His role on that expedition was more of a general servant, and

Figure 70   Henson on Board the SS *Roosevelt*. Everyone who worked with Henson described him in glowing terms, representative of the high regard they had for him.

he was not part of the sledging team that set off across the ice cap in 1892, but he did begin to acquire the skills that would be so important to the rest of his career. Most critically, he spent a considerable amount of time with the various Inughuit hunters who visited or worked with the expedition.

Henson returned to Greenland in 1893 and was on every one of Peary's trips after that. As Henson gained skills and became more fluent in Inuktitut, Peary relied on him more and more. Over the years, "Maripaluk," as the Inughuit called him (usually translated as "kind Matthew"), became increasingly integrated into the Inughuit community. In 1893, one of his first acts on arriving was to adopt an orphaned boy, Kudluktoq. By 1900, Henson had an Inughuit wife who was with him, Peary, and a small group of Inughuit men and women at Fort Conger on Ellesmere Island. Little is known about this young woman apart from her name, Elatu, and that she was ill off and on through the fall of 1900 with what the expedition doctor, Dr. Dedrick, diagnosed as possibly a liver or kidney ailment. She died in January 1901 and was buried at Fort Conger. Henson was devastated by her death, but he eventually overcame his grief. When he returned to Greenland in 1905, he began a relationship with a second Inughuit woman, Aqattanguaq, who was the mother of his only child, Anaukaq. Their descendants in the community still tell stories of the couple's loving, joking relationship.

Henson's status among the Inughuit as "nearly" one of them positioned him as the ideal intermediary between Peary and the men and women he hired, able to communicate Peary's goals to them more effectively than Peary himself could. In the North, Henson, with his many talents, was clearly one of the most important members of the expedition. However, when they returned to New York in 1909, Matthew Henson was treated differently from other members of Peary's team. Racism in America led many people to undervalue his accomplishments and his vital role on the expedition. He was excluded from most celebratory banquets, and honors given to the other men were not extended to him. Although the African American community in New York and elsewhere was quick to celebrate Henson, the racist policies of the time meant he was prohibited from even attending the many banquets thrown for Peary and the other men (although there are reports that Borup and MacMillan tried to sneak Henson into at least one New York celebration by dressing him up as a visiting Arab dignitary).

Emma Bonanomi has explored how deeply ingrained attitudes toward race in America in the early twentieth century impacted the way Henson was received on his return from the Pole. White people struggled with conflicting views of him as inferior due to his race but an American hero due to his accomplishments. She has shown how these conflicting attitudes played out when Henson began a lecture tour in the fall of 1909. Newspaper reports variously describe the mostly white audiences as both heckling and admiring, depending in part on the attitude of the writer. Henson launched himself on this national tour as a way to raise money, as his many years of work with Peary had been far from lucrative and left him with no permanent job. In doing so, however, he alienated Peary, who had insisted that none of the men publish their accounts or give public lectures until his own book was released. Although Peary ultimately agreed to write a preface to Henson's account of the expedition, published in 1912, they remained estranged.

It was many years before Henson received the recognition he deserved. In a thoughtful discussion of his life, historian Deirdre Stam describes

Figure 71   Delayed Recognition. While white members of the North Pole expedition received many awards on their return, Henson was frequently excluded. After many years of lobbying by Arctic explorers such as Donald MacMillan and Vilhjalmur Stefansson, organizations such as the Chicago Geographical Society awarded Henson the medals and honors that other members of the expedition had previously received.

numerous failed attempts in the late 1920s and early 1930s to grant him a federal pension. Over the years he did receive scattered honors, from an honorary degree from Howard University in 1939 to a gold medal from the Chicago Geographical Society in 1948 and an official citation from President Dwight Eisenhower in 1954. Henson died in New York City in 1955. He was buried there, with his American wife Lucy, whom he had married after returning from the North Pole. In 1988, through the efforts of S. Allen Counter, their remains were moved to Arlington National Cemetery and placed alongside those of Robert and Josephine Peary.

HENSON MEMORABILIA

Polar exploration loomed large in the public imagination in the early twentieth century, and makers of souvenirs and memorabilia took advantage of this interest to create all manner of items. Henson appears very rarely in the memorabilia, especially early on, but he was the only assistant, and the only African American, included in a trading card series called "World's Greatest Explorers" issued by the Hassan Tobacco company between 1910 and 1914. The cards were created by artist Albert Operti, who had traveled to Greenland with Peary and Henson in the 1890s. We can speculate that his first-hand experience with Henson led Operti to recognize Henson's important role, which is why he included Henson in the series. Captain Robert Bartlett was featured in the series as well.

MATTHEW A. HENSON

Figure 72   Hassan Cigarette Card, Matthew A. Henson.

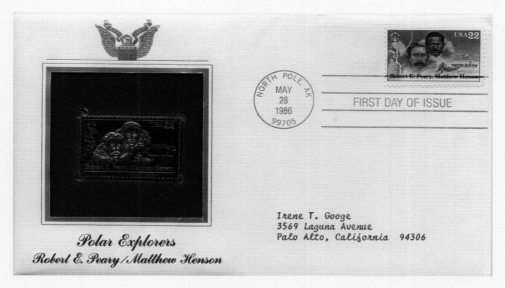

Figure 73   First Day Cover, Polar Explorers Stamp.

More recently, Henson has received additional attention. In 1969 he was profiled in a *Golden Legacy: Illustrated History Magazine*, and in 1986 he was given equal billing with Peary on a U.S. postage stamp, part of a series featuring Arctic explorers. He has been the subject of numerous children's books as well.

Robert Abram Bartlett

Robert Bartlett ("Captain Bob," as he came to be called) was descended from a long line of Newfoundland seafarers, many of them recognized for their work in the North. Peary came to know him in 1898, when Bartlett was mate on the *Windward*, captained by his uncle John Bartlett. Although the ship was supposed to return south after leaving Peary in the Arctic, it was iced in and so wintered at Payer Harbour. During this year in the North, Bartlett was affected by the "polar poison" (as he called it in his book, *The Log of Bob Bartlett*). While helping Peary, he learned from the Inughuit how to drive a dog sledge, how to keep warm, and generally how to survive in the North. In the process, he decided that Arctic work suited him well.

When Bartlett returned to Newfoundland in the fall of 1900, he did not have the opportunity of devoting himself to Arctic work right away—his uncles John and Sam Bartlett were still the captains of choice, at least for Peary and his associates. Between 1900 and 1905, Bob worked in the

Figure 74 Robert Abram Bartlett. As captain of the SS *Roosevelt*, Bartlett's primary responsibility was to oversee all operations of the vessel. But he also took part in all aspects of the expedition. Here he is relaxing on a break during a summer hunting expedition on Littleton Island, just north of Etah, before he began forcing the *Roosevelt* through the ice to Cape Sheridan. Once there, he took part in sledging expeditions to lay in caches, as well as hunting trips. While he was away, the mate, Tom Gushue, took charge of the ship.

sealing industry as captain of various vessels that carried sealers into the pack ice to harvest harp seals in the spring. During this time his uncle John called upon him once again in the summer of 1901 for a brief trip north aboard the *Algerine*, carrying a group of young American men to Hudson Bay for a hunting expedition. He was more than ready for a change in 1905, when Peary called upon him to take charge of his new exploration ship, the SS *Roosevelt*.

In addition to a love of the Arctic, Bartlett shared with Peary a determination that would be essential if they were to succeed. Peary chose Bartlett for his "youth and ambition," as well as his lineage, and in spite of his relatively limited experience as a captain (Bartlett was only 30 years old in 1905). If there were any doubts about Bartlett's suitability for the job, the 1905–1906 expedition put them to rest. On the voyage north, Bartlett forced the *Roosevelt* through the heavy pack ice of Kane

Basin and Robeson Channel, all the way to the relative safety of Cape Sheridan. In many ways, however, it was the voyage home at the helm of the crippled vessel that tested his seafaring skills. It was, in the words of David Nutt (himself an Arctic researcher and seafarer of note), "an epic of seamanship."

Despite the trials of what Bartlett described as "the hardest year of my life," he was eager to set off once again in 1908, having spent the intervening time helping Peary oversee repairs and modifications to the *Roosevelt*. The 1908 trip north was less eventful—the changes they had made to the *Roosevelt*, as well as better luck with the ice, made for an easier trip, although the ice still posed challenges. Bartlett drove the ship as far north as possible, arriving at Cape Sheridan on September 5. Taking advantage of a sliver of open water past Cape Sheridan, he steamed on for two more miles to set a new farthest north record for a vessel under power (surpassed only by the *Fram*, which was carried drifting, frozen into the ice of the Arctic Ocean) before returning to the relative safety of their familiar winter quarters.

Once again Bartlett was a key member of the sledging expeditions as they began the work of transporting supplies to Cape Columbia. In late February, he led the way onto the sea ice, charged with the daunting task of breaking trail for much of the trip. On April 1, his was the last party to turn back, leaving Peary, Henson, Odaq, Sigluk, Ukkaujaaq, and Iggianguaq to go on to the Pole. That morning, he set off north by himself, hoping to cross the 88th parallel as his own personal "farthest north." He walked five miles, took an observation, and returned to their camp. There, calculating his location, he discovered he had reached only 87°47' North, a result of the southward drift of the ice. He was, by all accounts, bitterly disappointed. Some accounts suggest that Peary had promised Bartlett that he would go all the way to the North Pole, although others claim Peary made no such promise to anyone. Many people have since wondered why Peary chose Henson over Bartlett, who could have provided a second navigational record of their location at the North Pole. There is no good evidence to say why Peary made this choice (he gave conflicting reasons), but Bartlett himself, as well as MacMillan and others, believed that it was because of Henson's unmatched skill as a dog-sledge driver and his vastly greater experience. The fact that Bartlett was British, not American, may have factored into Peary's decision as well. It was a fateful decision, as it turned out, given the later controversy about why Peary had not taken another white man to the Pole. He did promise Bartlett that he would be part of a future trip to the South Pole (he also invited MacMillan and Borup), but this venture never materialized.

On his return from the North Pole expedition, Bartlett was a celebrity, despite not having gone to the Pole itself, but he did not rest on his laurels. In 1910, he returned north at the helm of the *Beothic*, which had been chartered by two wealthy men, Harry Whitney and Paul Rainey, for a hunting trip. He continued sealing (without much success) and in 1913 accepted a position as the captain of the *Karluk* for the Canadian Arctic Expedition. The story of this disastrous voyage has been told many times by Bartlett himself, and later by a number of others. Bartlett's heroism when the ship, which had been locked in the ice for months, sank in January 1914 was widely celebrated, adding to his fame. The following years were difficult, however, and it was not until 1924 that he really found his feet again. That year a gift from a generous benefactor made it possible for him to purchase his own ship, the *Effie M. Morrissey*. At the helm of the "Little *Morrissey*," as he often called it, Bartlett sailed north again every year until 1945, carrying scientists, cinematographers, and (during the Second World War) supplies for military bases. His star rose once more in the public eye, and on many of these trips he had a Pathé News cameraman along as well, documenting their adventures for newsreels.

Bartlett remained close to the Peary family, and in 1932 he worked with Marie to construct a monument to Peary's memory at Cape York in northern Greenland. They departed from Eagle Island that summer, stopping in Newfoundland to pick up stone masons. Over the course of three months, with the help of many Inughuit, they quarried rock and constructed a 60-foot-tall triangular pillar, the apex pointing north, with two Ps inset on the sides, and topped with a 500-pound stainless steel cap. The monument still stands today.

Marie Peary, with her own links to the North, was an exception to Bartlett's strong prohibition against women on his ship. In 1941, the U.S. government asked him to take another woman north: the adventurer and researcher Louise Boyd. This was a much less happy voyage, as the two personalities clashed over most aspects of the trip. But it was an important voyage to the shores of northeastern Greenland, where Boyd, under cover of a geological study, was secretly investigating the source of radio interference in transatlantic communications vital to the war effort.

Figure 75   Peary Monument. During the construction of the Peary Monument in 1932, Bartlett hired many Inughuit to help and took the opportunity to visit old friends. Here Qisuk, Odaq, Bartlett, an unidentified Inughuit woman, and Marie stand in front of the completed monument before unveiling the dedication plaque. These events were captured by a Pathé News cameraman to be included in newsreels shown in cinemas around the country.

Bartlett died of pneumonia in New York City in 1946 and is buried in his hometown of Brigus, Newfoundland.

The Assistants

> *As to the quality of the personnel of a polar expedition, my*
> *experience has proved over and over again the accuracy of*
> *my theory that it should be made up wholly of young men, of*
> *first-class physique, perfect health, education, and attainment.*
>
> —Robert E. Peary, *The Secrets of Polar Travel*

Throughout his career Peary employed a series of young men, mostly Americans, to work with him in the field, always selecting for the qualities described above (and which could have described him in his youth). By and large, this selection method served him well. For the 1908–1909 expedition, he hired four young(ish) men to serve as leaders of the sledging parties (in addition to Henson and Bartlett). One of these, Ross Marvin, was a veteran of the 1905–1906 expedition, while the others were "tenderfeet" who had never been north.

Marvin had proved his mettle in 1905–1906, spending nearly two months with a small group of Inughuit hunting around Lake Hazen, in addition to being an active member of the sledging teams on the aborted trip to the North Pole and later exploratory trips. On top of these activities, he had taken responsibility for monitoring weather instruments and acted as Peary's secretary. Marvin was a last-minute addition to the 1908–1909 team, according to MacMillan, who described how a visit to bid the team farewell turned into an offer to join them. Once on board the *Roosevelt*, Marvin took up his old role as Peary's secretary and chief assistant, leading one of the key sledging teams and being one of the last teams to turn back. He was to return to the *Roosevelt* and then, with MacMillan, set off for Cape Morris Jesup, at the northernmost tip of Greenland, to collect a series of tidal readings and soundings. Sadly, Marvin never made it back to the ship. All of the men felt his loss, but Peary was particularly stricken. Marvin was only the second man to lose his life while working for Peary (the first being John Verhoeff, who had disappeared while traveling alone overland between Robertson and MacCormick Fjords in the spring of 1892). The men created a monument to Marvin at Cape Sheridan, which still stands today.

After Marvin's death, Donald B. MacMillan ably stepped in as chief assistant. MacMillan had all the qualities Peary was looking for in his assistants, including strength, stamina, a love of outdoor work, and a good education. Peary had first asked MacMillan to join his team in 1905, but MacMillan regretfully declined, feeling he had to honor his recently signed contract to teach at Worcester Academy. He was thrilled when, in the spring of 1908, Peary asked him to join the 1908–1909 expedition and accepted the offer immediately.

MacMillan decided to continue with the trip to Cape Morris Jesup to do the work Peary had requested of Marvin (including laying in food caches in case any of the teams ended up on the Greenland coast as they had in 1906), and he asked Borup to join him. Together the two "tenderfeet" planned the trip, from the number of sledges and dogs to the amount of food they would require on the 600-mile round trip. They left the *Roosevelt* on April 19 with five Inughuit men. Remarkably, despite their relative inexperience, the trip went well. As MacMillan said in a 1910 lecture, "Borup and myself, two inexperienced men, but with commander's perfect equipment were passing old world records and having the time of our lives." The presence of five Inughuit hunters was a major factor in their success, but they had indeed learned critical skills from both their Inughuit teachers and Peary.

MacMillan remained staunchly loyal to Peary throughout his life. He put the lessons he had learned to good use as he embarked on his own career as an Arctic explorer. He never returned to his position at Worcester Academy, instead leading his own expeditions to the Arctic until his retirement in 1954.

George Borup was the youngest member of the team, only 24 years old and recently graduated from Yale University. By all accounts, what he lacked in experience he made up for in enthusiasm, and, like MacMillan, he took well to the hard work Peary demanded of all of them. In addition

Figure 76 Tenderfeet at the Top of the World. This image, probably taken by Kudluktoq, shows Borup, MacMillan, and Qaajuuttaq posing at the cairn build by James Lockwood and David Brainard at their "farthest north" point, reached in 1882 as part of the Lady Franklin Bay expedition. Lockwood and Brainard set a record for the time, reaching 83°23.8' North, and then turned back, as they were running short of food and the spring snow was making travel increasingly difficult. MacMillan and Borup had no such troubles and continued on to Cape Morris Jesup, the most northerly point of Greenland.

to his duties as a member of the sledging teams, Borup was often responsible for some of the expedition photography, particularly developing many of the memorable images. On the polar trip he went farther than any of the other "tenderfeet," turning back at 85°23' North. After he and MacMillan returned from Cape Morris Jesup, Peary sent him out again, this time with instructions to build a memorial cairn at Cape Columbia, with an elaborate sign post constructed by Wardwell. He accomplished that task, although not before returning to the ship early with a live muskox calf they had captured. Sadly, the calf did not survive many days on board the ship.

Borup, like MacMillan, had been bitten by the Arctic bug, and when they returned to the United States he was eager to embark on his newfound career. Peary had invited him to be part of the proposed expedition to the South Pole, but first the controversy, and then Roald Amundsen's successful Antarctic expedition, ruled that out. Instead, Borup and MacMillan planned their own jointly led expedition to determine whether Crocker Land, an area that Peary had sighted from Cape Thomas Hubbard in 1906, actually existed. This would be more than simply exploration, however. It would be an ambitious scientific expedition as well. Peary supported their efforts and seems to have been particularly fond of Borup, inviting him to visit with his family on different occasions. This led to a romance between Borup and Marie, although surviving correspondence indicates that while Borup was infatuated with Marie, she was less excited about the relationship.

Figure 77   Monument at Cape Columbia. Borup, Ukkaujaaq, and Sigluk constructed this large cairn at Cape Columbia to commemorate the North Pole expedition. One arm of the sign bore the name of the location, while the others pointed toward and named the farthest north, east, and west that expedition members had traveled, including the date they had been there and the distance. A plaque described the expedition and listed all the members of the crew.

Tragically, in April 1912, less than two months before he and MacMillan were to leave on the Crocker Land Expedition, Borup drowned in a canoeing accident. Marie wrote after his death that she "loved him dearly, tho not in the way he wished." His loss was indeed a great tragedy for everyone who knew him. As John Goodsell wrote, "During dark and trying periods, he was always a morale builder with his quick wit and ever-present enthusiasm."

Goodsell was the last of the "tenderfeet" on the expedition, and for the most part he also fit into Peary's concept of the ideal assistant. He was not as young as the others, nor as athletic, but his qualification as a medical doctor overrode these considerations. Peary always included a physician on his trips to attend to the inevitable strains, injuries, and illnesses that the men would incur. Goodsell accomplished this and more, learning with the others to drive dog sledges, taking part in hunting trips, laying in food caches, and participating in the early parts of the North Pole journey itself. According to MacMillan, Goodsell "was a bit too heavy and slow for sledging, but a bulldog in determination and stoical to the

Figure 78   Dr. John Goodsell.
Despite being older and heavier than Peary's ideal assistant, Dr. John Goodsell worked as hard as any of the others on the trail, all the while looking after their medical needs. He cared for all the members of the expedition, from men injured in shipboard accidents or suffering from frostbite to newborn infants. Although he found sledging difficult, he nurtured hope of returning to the North until after the First World War, when a heart ailment made such work impossible.

last degree." He was the first of the assistants that Peary sent back to land, along with two ailing Inughuit men. After his return from sledging in March, Goodsell spent most of his time at Cape Sheridan, tending to the medical needs of the people there. In June, however, he managed to get away for a short time to collect specimens from Lake Hazen and to visit Fort Conger, where he met up with MacMillan, who was taking a series of tidal readings.

Goodsell's participation in the expedition was generally successful, but once back in the south his feelings toward Peary soured. When they signed on to the expedition, all of the men had agreed to give Peary access to their journals and photographs and to refrain from lecturing or publishing about their experiences until his account had been published. (These sorts of restrictions were common at the time.) In the media frenzy that followed their return, however, these strictures were tested. Goodsell felt that Peary had taken a dislike to him and treated him differently from the other men. His posthumously published account of the expedition ends with a long litany of complaints about Peary—some petty, others more serious.

Without Peary's side of the story, it is difficult to evaluate many of Goodsell's accusations, but Peary does seem to have treated him badly. One of Goodsell's claims—that Peary copied liberally and directly from Goodsell's journals when writing his expedition account—is likely true, although it was not Peary who did the copying. *The North Pole* was largely ghostwritten by A. E. Thomas, and numerous authors have documented the difficulty that Thomas had in working with Peary, the result being that the book is indeed based in large part on the journals of the other men. In 1915, Goodsell finally had a manuscript ready for publication. He sent it to Peary, asking for his approval to publish it and that he write an introduction, as he had done for others. Peary seems to have sat on the manuscript for eight months, returning it unopened and unread, claiming that it had been left on Eagle Island over the winter. Donald Whisenhunt and Anita Genger, who prepared Goodsell's manuscript for publication in 1983, describe a series of letters between Goodsell and the Explorers Club (which he had asked to intervene) in which the matter escalates until Goodsell as much as accuses Peary of lying about the manuscript. They had essentially no contact after this exchange. Goodsell died in 1949, his account of his experiences unpublished.

. . . Even If He Wished He Could

Peary's treatment of Goodsell, while perhaps not quite as cavalier and callous as Goodsell claimed, was in some ways characteristic. Henson experienced much the same treatment, despite their long and productive association. In Henson's case, many have suggested that Peary shunned him because he could substantiate claims that Peary had faked their reaching of the North Pole. It is possible that there is a grain of truth in such speculations, but it is important to recognize that, independent of any possible cover-up of fraudulent claims, Peary's behavior toward Henson fits into a well-established pattern, exacerbated in this case by racism. He demanded hard work and loyalty from those who worked for him, but these qualities alone were not sufficient to guarantee Peary's long-term support.

Historian Lyle Dick has characterized Peary's attitude (in this case toward Inughuit women) as "instrumentalist," and in many ways this is an apt description. To some degree he saw those who worked for him as a means to an end, and once he no longer needed their services, they were not his concern. This is not true of everyone who worked for him—he maintained relationships with some of the men, notably Bartlett, Borup, and MacMillan, and they reciprocated with a fierce loyalty to him, as did his family. But Peary was without a doubt a difficult and complicated person. In his writing he gives those who helped him credit but always makes it clear that the main enterprise, and the success of it, was his alone.

5

PEARY AND THE INUGHUIT

In 2011, the authors traveled to Cape Sheridan to investigate the remains of the shore-based living accommodations left there by members of Peary's 1905–1906 and 1908–1909 expeditions. These had first been studied by archaeologists working for Parks Canada in the 1970s but had not been visited since, and we felt it was time to reevaluate the situation. We were particularly interested in recording evidence of the Inughuit families that had lived there. Although they were vital to the success of Peary's work, their roles are often neglected and the Inughuit left no written accounts of their own to describe their experiences. We learn about them through the writings of Peary and his men and a few others who recorded Inughuit stories they had heard, but these are inevitably colored by the deeply ingrained racist and sexist attitudes of their time. We also glean some information about Inughuit expedition participants from studying the Westerners' photographs. Archaeology is one of the few ways we have of learning about their experiences through a different lens.

Floeberg Beach is a bleak place. The only people who ever chose to live there were explorers—first Captain George Nares and the crew of the HMS *Alert*, who wintered there in 1875–1876, and then Peary and his teams. There is no evidence that any Inuit except those working for Peary ever settled there, and even today it is visited only occasionally by residents of the nearby Canadian Forces Station Alert (and even less frequently by adventure travelers). And yet, on two occasions, while working for Peary, a group of Inughuit families did make their home here, far from the familiar shores of Smith Sound and their extended families. How they coped is a testament to their resilience and determination.

Figure 79 Archaeology at Floeberg Beach. Frédéric Dussault excavates the remains of an Inughuit snow house, while in the background the authors excavate in the remains of two of the crate houses constructed during the 1908–1909 expedition. Between them the ground surface has been disturbed by tracked vehicles from the nearby Canadian Forces Station Alert. Elsewhere on the beach are the remains of 15 Inughuit tent rings, from the 1905–1906 and 1908–1909 expeditions.

Who Are the Inughuit?

The Inughuit are the indigenous people of northwestern Greenland. Traditionally, Inughuit lived in small seasonal communities along the shores of Smith Sound and Kane Basin, from Cape York in the south to Inglefield Land in the north. Today they live in a few settled communities, including Qaanaaq (the administrative center) and Siorapaluk (the most northerly indigenous village in the world). They speak Inuktun (a dialect of Inuktitut) and are closely related to Inuit groups in the rest of Greenland, Canada, and Alaska. Inughuit—their name for themselves—means "the people." In the past they were sometimes referred to as Polar Inuit, or Polar Eskimos, or the Smith Sound Eskimos, which is how Peary usually identified them.

In 1891, when Peary first traveled to Smith Sound, the Inughuit were living very much as their ancestors had: in small seasonal settlements, moving to take advantage of the resources available at different times of the year. In winter, families lived in warm houses partially dug into the ground, with walls and roofs of stone and sod blocks, insulated with snow. Inside a house, the floor was carefully paved with flat stones, and the back of the house was taken up by a raised platform, which served as a sitting and sleeping area and was cushioned with heather and furs. In front of the platform, at one or both sides, was a stand to hold a stone lamp that burned seal or whale oil, the only source of heat and light in the house. The woman (or women) of the house could easily reach the lamp from her spot on the sleeping platform, keeping the lamp burning at all times. Sod houses were permanent, used each winter for many years, although not necessarily by the same family. In spring, when these houses became too damp to be pleasant, the family moved out, taking the roof off so the house could air out over the summer. In summer, they lived in seal-skin tents. In the fall, they would decide where they wanted to spend the winter and then claim one of the houses, clean it up, and put the roof back on it, so it would be ready for another winter. They also used snow houses in winter when necessary while out traveling or hunting, but they did not live in these houses for long periods.

The Inughuit economy depended largely on hunting sea mammals such as seals, walrus, and narwhal, using the sea ice as a platform for hunting

Figure 80 Winter House. Winter houses were partly dug into the ground or into the side of a hill, taking advantage of the ground to help insulate them. Often, they were outfitted with a window fashioned from thinly split skin or strips of sea mammal intestines sewn together. The areas in front of sod houses became activity areas, places where people socialized and worked, and where women aired out the family's clothing.

Figure 81   Tent. Women sewed tents out of sealskin. In the past, some women were so skilled that they could split the skins used for the front of the tent to thin them, allowing more light to penetrate the tent interior. Over the short summer, however, most activities took place outside.

Figure 82   Snow House. Snow is an excellent insulator, and a house built out of snow can be relatively warm and quiet, even in the midst of a blizzard. Inside, there would be a sleeping platform just like in a sod house, taking advantage of the way warm air rises. Inughuit used snow houses primarily when they were traveling, however, preferring to stay in a sod and stone house if one was available.

and a highway for travel. The Smith Sound region is rich in marine life, thanks to a phenomenon known as the North Water Polynya. This is an area where wind and currents keep ice from forming even in the depths of winter. Marine mammals and sea birds are attracted to this open water, making it an ideal place for hunters, too. Inughuit also hunted caribou and muskox, trapped foxes and Arctic hares, and in the summer netted large numbers of birds (mostly dovekies) and collected bird eggs. They constructed stone caches to store excess meat caught in times of plenty for use during times when hunting was difficult. Extended periods of stormy weather could keep hunters at home, for example, especially in the winter. As with most hunting societies, the Inughuit did suffer periods of stress and even famine.

The community was held together by familial ties. A man and a woman were the fundamental unit of survival. Typically, men hunted large animals, an often dangerous occupation that could take them away from home for days at a time. They also made all their tools and weapons as well as sledges and kayaks. Women managed the household, including caring for children and hunting, trapping, or catching smaller animals,

Figure 83   Pulling in Narwhal. Sea mammals provided most of the food and fuel that Inughuit families consumed, as well as food for their dogs, skins and sinew for clothing, and ivory for tools. The meat was and continues to be eaten fresh, dried, or frozen for later use. The skin and blubber of whales, *mattaq*, continues to be a particular favorite. Seal and walrus skin was not eaten but cleaned and used for clothing, tents, kayak covers, and ropes and lashings. The blubber was eaten or rendered into oil to fuel the lamps. Sinew from narwhals was cleaned and dried to be used for sewing thread. Bones and ivory were carved into numerous different tools and ornaments.

Figure 84   Netting Birds. Men, women, and children all netted birds during the summer. It could be dangerous work, however, as there was always the danger of falling off the steep, rocky cliffs where the birds nest. Some birds would be eaten fresh, but most would be preserved for the winter. Inughuit families would fill sacks made from whole sealskins with hundreds of birds and store them in caches for months, allowing them to ferment into a delicacy called *kiviak*, with a taste similar to that of a strong cheese. The skins of fresh birds were used to sew warm underclothing as well.

Figure 85   Hunting. Men hunted various species, using different techniques, and in different places, depending on the time of year. Polar bears, for example, were hunted in spring when people went on days- or weeks-long trips to the north end of Smith Sound or far off-shore by Cape York. Seals, one of the mainstays of their diet, could be caught at the animals' breathing holes in the winter or stalked as they basked on the ice in the spring. Walrus and narwhal were pursued at the ice edge or in open water, from kayaks. Caribou were hunted in the late summer and early fall, when their coats were at their best for making clothing.

birds, and fish. They also tended the stone lamps that were the only source of light and heat for warmth, drying wet garments, and cooking. A large part of women's time was spent cleaning hides of the animals they and their husbands caught and sewing them into all the clothing and footwear that their family needed. Without the warm and waterproof clothing that women made, men would be unable to hunt, and without the animals the men hunted, women would not be able to make clothing. Neither would survive long without the other. As Knud Rasmussen put it in 1921, "It is not without reason that the Polar Eskimo says that a man, as hunter, is what his wife makes of him."

As is usually the case for small scale hunting societies, there was no permanent leader among the Inughuit. When a group of men hunted cooperatively, the best hunter might act as leader, but this position did not necessarily translate into a leadership role in other situations. On the contrary, individual autonomy (especially for men) was far more important. Disagreements between individuals or families might be resolved by one side simply moving elsewhere—no one had the authority to force any other person to do something they did not want to do. More important than individual autonomy, however, was the survival of the group. Nuclear and extended families worked together and shared resources.

The Inughuit first encountered Europeans in 1818, when Captain John Ross of the Royal Navy sailed up Baffin Bay to Cape York and met a group of hunters. Ross had with him a Greenlandic Inuk, Hans Sacheuse, who acted as interpreter. Through him, the Inughuit told Ross a bit about their lives, including the fact that they did not hunt with bows and arrows or use kayaks. According to their oral history, these technologies were lost when most of the population died in an epidemic. Ross published the first written description of the Inughuit, and from the 1820s onward, whalers and occasional exploration parties ventured to Cape York in the summer. These visitors brought with them a small and unreliable stream of highly desirable trade goods, including wood and industrial iron to supplement the locally available meteoric iron the Inughuit used. Inughuit families are said to have traveled to the southern part of Smith Sound in the summer in the hope that they could trade with these visitors. In the 1860s, the Inughuit community, thought by some to be shrinking, was invigorated by new visitors. A small group of Inuit under the leadership of the shaman Qitdlarsuaq migrated to the Smith Sound region from northern Baffin Island. These Inuit brought with them their kayaks and bows and arrows

Figures 86 and 87   Lamp. Women tended lamps fueled by oil rendered from sea mammal blubber, most often seal but also narwhal and even walrus. The shallow stone lamps were the only source of both heat and light during the very long, dark winter. Without the lamp, there would be no way to melt snow and ice for drinking water, no way to dry damp clothing, no way to cook food, and no way to heat the house or illuminate it. A woman's skill at keeping a smoke-free flame burning at all times was an important measure of her abilities in general.

Figure 88   Scraping and Sewing. Women were always engaged in sewing or cleaning hides in preparation for sewing. They began learning these skills as children, helping to clean hides and making clothing for dolls by copying their mothers, aunts, and grandmothers. Before a girl married, she would be able to make all the articles of clothing her family would need, from waterproof boots to beautiful parkas. Women faced a constant battle to repair or replace worn garments, but they took the time to ensure that the clothing they sewed was both functional and beautiful.

and reintroduced these important tools to the Inughuit. Some of these migrants married into Inughuit families, and many people in the community today can trace their ancestry to the migrants.

Peary and the Inughuit

Peary was not the first American to spend time with the Inughuit, but he spent far more time with them than anyone before him. In 1853–1855, the American explorer Elisha Kent Kane wintered in Smith Sound. He wrote

Figure 89   An Extended Family. (Back l-r) Qaaviguaq, Ittukusuk, Amaunalik, Qarkutsiaq, Kuutsikitoq. (Front l-r) Qaijunguaq, Ane holding Ole, Atangana with Inatdliaq on her back, and Aviaq. Family ties linked individuals and groups across the small community, and they often guided people's choices about where to live and with whom to hunt. Donald MacMillan took this photograph of the members of two extended families who worked with him in 1923–1924. Most of them are the children of men who had worked on the 1908–1909 expedition. Two brothers, Ittukusuk and Qarkutsiaq, were the sons of Panikpak, who had worked with Peary. Qarkutsiaq's wife, Atangana (with their daughter Inatdliaq on her back), and her sister Aviaq were also there, as was their adopted daughter, Qaijunguaq. Aviaq later married Anaukaq Henson. Ittukusuk's wife Ane holds their son, Ole. Aviaq and Anaukaq fostered Ole after his father died. Kuutsikitoq was Odaq's son. His cousin Amaunalik and her husband Qaaviguaq also worked with MacMillan.

a very popular book about his experiences, including descriptions of the Inughuit. Other expeditions followed, all resulting in books with descriptions of explorers' interactions with Inughuit families. Peary had read all of these before he ever visited Greenland, so he had some idea of what to expect when he arrived. He already knew that he had much to learn from the Inughuit about surviving in the North, but at the same time, as a typical college-educated nineteenth-century man, his expectations were filtered through both his own cultural biases and those of the authors whose books he had read. His writings betray a sometimes romantic and stereotypical view of the Inughuit, and although he admired them in many ways, he certainly did not view them as equals.

In spite of his prejudices, Peary was heavily dependent on Inughuit knowledge and skills, and he knew it. Conversely, while they had many incentives to work for Peary, ultimately they could get along without him and the trade goods he provided in payment for their labor and expertise. Over the many years they worked together, Peary and the Inughuit were involved in a very complex relationship, and although Peary was well aware of how important the Inughuit men and women were to him, and frequently commented on it in his writing, today their role in his success frequently goes unrecognized.

Peary's first encounter with Inughuit came in 1891. As soon as the expedition house, Red Cliff House, was completed, he sent some of the men off in a small boat to look for an Inughuit community, to trade for ethnographic specimens to bring home, and to try to entice a family to come and work for the expedition. He gave his men the authority to offer one lucky hunter the use of a rifle for the duration of employment. Despite the language barrier, Peary's men had little difficulty communicating Peary's wishes, and they returned with a family: the hunter Equ, his wife Mannik, and their two children, who stayed at Red Cliff House for the remainder of the year.

Tellingly, Peary writes that during that year Equ and Mannik returned to their community only for brief visits, "in order, as we afterwards learned, to air their importance and exhibit the wealth they had newly acquired from the white men." While this statement is no doubt an exaggeration, it probably contains a germ of truth, in that trade goods were highly desirable. It is also a good indication of Peary's inflated sense of his beneficial impact on the community. During the next few months, many more Inughuit came to see these new strangers, to visit, to trade, and to work, staying for days or months at a time, some establishing what would become long-term relationships with Peary. Over the next 18 years, this pattern continued—Peary needed help and was willing to pay for it, while the Inughuit provided assistance in exchange for trade goods.

It is hard to overstate how dependent Peary was on the Inughuit. Much of his success is directly attributable to the labor, knowledge, and skills of Inughuit men and women. Among the most important was the clothing his men wore, expertly made by Inughuit women. The women who worked for Peary used a combination of traditional and imported materials to make expedition clothing that was far superior to anything made in the south. Over thousands of years, northern women had developed styles of

Figures 90–92   Men on Sledge, Caribou-Skin Parka, Polar Bear Pants. Inughuit women tailored clothing for their husbands and sons, ensuring that pants had a snug fit just below the knee, with an adjustable, low-slung waist. According to Peary, a pair of polar bear pants was ideal, "impervious to cold . . . almost indestructible." They had different parkas for different conditions, as seen in the top photo. Standing on the left and right, Donald MacMillan and Tom Gushue wear caribou fur parkas. These are too warm for strenuous work, even in the coldest conditions, but the men used them in camp and even slept in them, simply drawing their arms inside. Between MacMillan and Gushue, George Borup wears a sheepskin parka. The men wore these lighter parkas on the trail, as they were less warm and so less likely to become too wet with sweat as the men maneuvered heavy sledges over ice ridges and across leads. Seated on the sledge, Matthew Henson wears a traditional fox fur parka, made for him by his Inughuit wife, Aqattanguaq.

clothing that made the best use of the materials available to them. From the choice of fur to the stitches used to sew them together, every aspect of the garments they made was carefully considered to ensure that the clothing functioned well. With expert eyes, they judged the size of each man and tailored parkas and pants to fit. Dr. John Goodsell, the surgeon on Peary's 1908–1909 expedition, was awed by the women's skills: "The women are so expert with the needle that the fur garments they make fit as though made by a professional tailor. They take very few measurements, depending largely upon the eye for estimating size."

Sledges and dogs (and the skills associated with them) were also an essential part of all of Peary's expeditions. He relied heavily on Inughuit men to manage them and to teach first him, and later his men, how to manage both. The sledges themselves were based on traditional Inughuit designs, as were the dog traces. The sledges were larger than traditional sledges, in line with the heavier loads they would carry, but managing them required the same skills utilized in handling the smaller sledges that Inughuit men built for their own use. However, with the exception of Henson, the Westerners were never as accomplished as their Inughuit teachers, so Peary typically sent his young assistants out with expert Inughuit men to advise them and keep them out of dangerous situations. This arrangement sometimes led to disagreements and misunderstandings. In his journal, George Borup wrote about a trip he made with two Inughuit men in the fall of 1908. One morning he felt they should be sledging, but the Inughuit men wanted to wait until there was more moonlight by which to see (the sun having set for the winter). According to Borup, they settled this disagreement with a "rough house" (presumably a friendly wrestling match) and got on with their work. Not all disagreements were so easily settled, as Ross Marvin's death in the spring of 1909 attests, but in general Peary's men were eager to learn from the Inughuit hunters and quickly came to appreciate their skills and knowledge.

Peary also depended on Inughuit hunters to supply his expeditions with fresh, local food whenever practical. Having fresh meat was important both for health reasons and for overall morale. On long sledging trips on the sea ice, men and dogs were forced to eat pemmican, but at all other times both preferred fresh, or frozen, meat. During the fall on his last two expeditions, Peary sent teams of Inughuit men and his American assistants out for days at a time to procure meat for the winter.

Figure 93   Hunting Party. Three Inughuit men working for Peary—Qaajuuttaq, Aleqasinnguaq, and Inukittoq—led John Goodsell (standing second from the left) and George Borup, who took this photograph, on one of their first hunting trips in the North, teaching them how to survive in the Arctic.

Once they were traveling on the sea ice, Peary and his men also relied on Inughuit hunters to construct snow houses, or igloos, resorting to canvas tents only when absolutely necessary. Snow houses are warm and sturdy, and they can be built quickly by an experienced hunter using wind-packed snow. A well-built snow house will last for many weeks, so the snow houses they constructed on the route from Cape Sheridan to Cape Columbia in 1908, for example, could be reused over and over by different teams. On the route to the Pole, igloos served as stopping places as well, and the fact that returning parties did not have to rebuild the shelters made it possible for the men to travel farther, often stopping briefly at one igloo in the middle of a march before setting off for the next igloo in which they slept. From the clothing they wore to the fresh meat they ate, and the great distances they traveled over the ice with relative ease, almost every element of Peary's success was based on Inughuit technology and dependent on their willingness to help him.

In the simplest terms, the relationship between Peary and the Inughuit who worked with him can be seen as a straightforward exchange—Peary needed labor and expertise, and the Inughuit needed (or wanted) the manufactured goods he could supply; thus, each stood to gain from the transaction. Peary considered the Inughuit among his most important supporters, and himself their great benefactor.

However, Peary's impact on the Inughuit was not nearly as beneficial as he believed. Understanding their complex relationship and the long-term impact of Peary's expeditions is challenging, not the least because we really only have one side of the story—Peary's. Only he and some of the men who worked for him have left first-hand written accounts of their experiences, and although they often write about the Inughuit men and women, their words are inevitably colored by the strongly held racist and sexist attitudes of their time. A close reading of Peary's writings and those of his men reveals levels of stress and social disruption among the Inughuit that are largely glossed over by Peary and others.

Economic Impact

In his 1917 book, *The Secrets of Polar Travel*, Peary congratulated himself for leaving the Inughuit better off than he had found them, and particularly for the fact that by 1909 every hunter in the group had a modern gun. Peary did not introduce the Inughuit to guns. That had happened decades earlier, and some had even traded well-used guns to him in the 1890s (now in the collection of the American Museum of Natural History), but he did provide many new guns in exchange for labor. Hunters were well aware of the advantages of firearms, and, as with Equ, the first hunter Peary hired in 1891, the promise of a new gun was a strong incentive to work for Peary. Men also traded for iron, steel, and knives and other tools, including sledge shoes.

Women, too, had incentive to work for Peary. Like all the explorers before him, he brought packets of steel needles, which made women's lives a bit easier as they sewed for their families and for the expedition. As with guns, steel needles were probably familiar to Inughuit women in the 1890s, but they were still valuable. Inughuit women clearly had a preference for items that were practical and useful to them in their everyday activities. Unlike women in other parts of the Arctic, Inughuit women were not interested in trading for beads or other "trinkets." Historic photographs show that they never decorated their clothing with beads (although for a short while some did use shell buttons), and in 1891 one elderly Inughuit woman even traded a small string of glass beads that she had received in 1871 to Langdon Gibson, a member of Peary's first expedition.

Figure 94 **Decoration.** Photographs taken in northwestern Greenland around the turn of the century show that some women sewed small white buttons onto their parkas as decoration, but they rarely, if ever, wore or sewed with colorful glass beads. Instead, they preferred to use contrasting colors of fur to make their clothing beautiful, as they had for generations.

Over the long term, these material goods do seem to have had a mostly positive impact on Inughuit society, although it cannot be attributed solely to Peary. Demographic studies show that the population began to grow around the time Peary's expeditions ended, and hunting patterns changed, partly because guns contributed to increased food security in a very difficult environment. But this success was not without costs, for while guns were highly desirable, they were also relatively expensive to use and maintain.

The hunters on Peary's expeditions could generally rely on him to provide ammunition, without which the guns were useless. Yet, after 1909, they needed another source. Knud Rasmussen, a Danish/Greenlandic explorer and anthropologist who had spent the winter of 1904–1905 in the area, saw the problem of access to goods and established the Thule trading station in 1910. The trading station ensured that there was a more or less steady supply of ammunition and other goods in the region. In return, people were expected to provide furs, particularly those of the valuable Arctic fox. This they did, making some adjustments to their hunting and trapping strategies. Rasmussen remained an influential force in the community until his untimely death in 1935, working with the hunters to establish regulations around hunting practices that ensured the preservation of traditional technologies. Even today Inughuit hunters continue to use dog-drawn sledges rather than snow machines and follow rules regarding the use of kayaks and harpoons, along with motor boats and guns, when hunting narwhal and walrus.

The hunting Peary and his men did, however, was a cause for concern in the following years and even decades. Historian Lyle Dick has noted that Peary's demand for hunted animals, combined with the skills and knowledge of the Inughuit hunters, effectively wiped out populations of muskox and caribou in areas of both Greenland and Ellesmere Island. Already by 1908 the men at Cape Sheridan were going farther afield than they had previously to provide meat for the expedition, due to overhunting in 1905–1906. Knud Rasmussen reports that caribou in the Thule district were essentially wiped out early in the twentieth century. Walrus populations were likewise impacted. Peary and his men hunted walrus extensively using open boats and guns, a method that was far more effective than the kayaks and harpoons Inughuit men had traditionally used. Each year they killed hundreds of walrus, some for themselves and their dogs, but also to establish caches of meat for the following winter, and to compensate hunters who spent time working for Peary when they would normally have been hunting for their families.

The impact of all this overhunting was not as dire for the Inughuit as it could have been, however. In the absence of caribou, hunters routinely traveled to Ellesmere Island to hunt muskox in the 1910s and 1920s and, as described above, also increased their hunting of marine mammals such as seals and narwhals. This practice ensured that their families and dog teams were fed and allowed the Inughuit population to begin to grow.

Social Stress

While the short- and long-term economic benefits that seem to have been the main incentive for the Inughuit to work for Peary were tangible and clearly important, they came at a significant cost. Today, Peary is often seen as having taken advantage of the people who worked for him, treating them poorly, paying them little for the arduous work, and disrupting the whole community socially and economically—quite the opposite of his own view of the matter, but perhaps closer to the truth than the rosy picture he presented.

Over the years, as Peary's expeditions increased in size, so, too, did the social disruption. While on his first expedition he worked primarily with one family, and no Inughuit accompanied him on his trip across the inland ice, by his last expeditions he was hiring many more people (22 men and 17 women, plus children) and transporting them all 300 miles away from their homes for nearly a year. This represented almost a quarter of the population and included some of the best hunters in the community. It is not possible to evaluate the impact of this practice on the people who stayed behind. Harry Whitney, a big-game hunter who spent the winter of 1908–1909 at Etah and nearby Anoritok, reports several periods of food scarcity that winter, but also many successful hunts. Given that families would normally be scattered to different places for the winter, it is possible that having so many people farther away than normal was not as much of a hardship as it might seem. The absence, however, of these families surely did have an impact—if not that year, then the next, when everyone returned to Greenland late in the summer, having missed much of the best time for hunting to store meat for the winter. Peary tried to make up for this lack of food with a massive walrus hunt, but it is unclear how successful this effort was.

Much of the stress under which Inughuit men and women worked is best understood on a personal, rather than community, level. Considering just the last two expeditions, the hardship was very real for those who lived at Cape Sheridan. The men in particular were often engaged in work that was both physically exhausting and dangerous. During the two years they spent there, the men were often hunting, much as they would have been at home, although, since the region around Cape Sheridan is not optimal for their preferred marine mammals, they primarily sought caribou and muskox. Much time was also spent ferrying supplies north in preparation for the journey to the Pole. But the weeks they spent on the sea ice were a different matter. Hacking a path through ridges of ice for long days at a time, under the constant threat of the ice breaking up, during the coldest part of the year, was work they would only engage in with Peary. It was physically demanding, and injuries were common. To make matters worse, they subsisted on a diet of pemmican, biscuits, condensed milk, and tea—a far cry from the food they were used to eating. They endured these conditions, but signs of stress were everywhere. Peary was aware of this reality at some level. When they were stopped at the Big Lead, for example, he recognized that the delay made the men nervous, and he was grateful that MacMillan organized games to distract them. But he rather angrily sent two men home when they asked to be released due to illness, disbelieving their complaints. This, despite the fact that one of them, Panikpak, had worked for him for many years, and both Dr. Goodsell and MacMillan were well aware that he had been struggling with a shoulder injury. Although Peary was not always without sympathy, he could be demanding and impatient with anyone who could not carry out their duty.

For the women working with Peary, there were other causes of stress. They had each other for support but were otherwise cut off from their extended family networks, living in an unfamiliar and inhospitable landscape. Although the expedition supplied them with food, the tinned rations were no substitute for the foods they were accustomed to having at home. Peary had expected them to live on board the *Roosevelt,* as his men did, but many found it too stifling. Their assigned quarters in the forecastle were crowded and dark and put them in close proximity to the men of the expedition, who were not above sexually harassing them. Instead, many chose to live in tents, snow houses, and huts built on shore. There they tried to maintain the familiar rhythms of life but faced additional challenges.

For Inughuit women, keeping house meant maintaining the seal oil lamp, which, in addition to being the only source of heat and light, represented an important symbolic link between a woman's care of the lamp's flame and the success of her husband's hunting. But at Cape Sheridan this proved very difficult. Women had their stone lamps with them but could not bring enough sea mammal oil to fuel them for the whole winter, and there was none to be had in their temporary community—the moving pack ice off Cape Sheridan is not good habitat for seals. Unable to use their traditional lamps, the women were forced to use ad hoc kerosene lamps constructed from old cans. These worked very differently from their traditional lamps and were probably both smellier and smokier. The differences in form, fuel, and use not only made heating and lighting their homes more difficult but also undermined women's symbolic role, adding significantly to the stresses they were experiencing.

Sexual harassment was a very real problem as well. Peary's attitude toward Inughuit women was complicated, but it is clear that he condoned, and even encouraged, sexual relationships between his men and local women, considering it important for the *men's* well-being. Lyle Dick has documented various episodes of sexual harassment recorded in the personal journals of men on Peary's expeditions. Most of the men who worked with Peary, either as assistants or as crew of the *Roosevelt*, were in the North for only a single expedition and understood little of the Inughuit language or culture. There is no evidence that any of them established long-term relationships with Inughuit women, but they certainly engaged in short-term liaisons.

Peary and Henson, by contrast, developed strong, loving relationships with women that persisted over many years. Peary's relationship with Aleqasina began during his 1893–1895 expedition and lasted until at least 1906, when their second son, Kali, was born. Historian Kenn Harper has noted that this was a complex relationship, which she and her Inughuit husband Piugattoq saw as a traditional wife-exchange partnership, although Peary may not have recognized this fact. He viewed Aleqasina affectionately but certainly did not think of her as the equal of either himself or Josephine. Henson also developed close attachments. During the 1898–1902 expedition, he appears to have been married to an Inughuit woman named Elatu, who tragically died of an unspecified ailment in January 1901. According to Peary, Henson was devastated by her death. By 1905, he had entered into a close relationship with Aqattanguaq, who bore him a son, Anaukaq—his only child. But these more or less stable relationships were the exception, and women working for the expedition had every reason to try to limit contact with the men aboard the ship.

One of the ways Inughuit women, and less often men, expressed their stress was through a phenomenon called *pibloktoq*, sometimes referred to as Arctic hysteria. During episodes of *pibloktoq*, sufferers behaved erratically and irrationally, singing loudly, often removing some or all of their clothes, and sometimes running off over the sea ice, forcing their friends and family to run after them and restrain them for fear that they would die of exposure. Lyle Dick has convincingly argued that this mysterious "disease" was a manifestation of psychological distress directly related to the difficult situation in which women found themselves. That the stress was at least in part related to working for the expedition can be seen by comparing the number of times American men at Cape Sheridan in 1908–1909 reported episodes of *pibloktoq* to the number that Harry Whitney reported over the same period in Greenland. In published and archival records, there were 29 reported incidents at Cape Sheridan, mostly in the fall. This is a dramatic under-representation of the actual numbers. In June 1909, George Wardwell reported an episode in his journal, writing that the women "have these spells so often I don't notice it now." Meanwhile, in Greenland, Whitney reported only four episodes. Women and men "at home" seem to have been much less vulnerable to this disorder and were, presumably, under considerably less stress.

Over the long term, despite the many stresses they endured while working for Peary, the Inughuit displayed a remarkable resilience and, as Lyle Dick put it, "the capacity . . . to turn an unfavorable situation to their own advantage." By working for Peary, some families earned a great deal, paid not in money but in useful goods. Materials that had been rare before, such as wood and steel, become much more common. In addition to material goods, the Inughuit learned a great deal about new technologies and used that knowledge to their advantage, selectively adopting materials that were useful to them, such as guns, while rejecting those that were not, such as kerosene lamps. Despite the years of disruption, they continued their traditional way of life as much as possible, using the industrial technology they adopted to reduce the seasonal insecurity they often faced.

The children that Peary and Henson left behind were raised by their Inughuit families and integrated into the community. Peary's older son, Anaukaq (later called Samik), died in 1927, leaving behind his own young son. Peary's younger son, Kali, lived to be 92 and has many descendants. Henson's son, Anaukaq, lived to be 81 and also has many descendants. Both Kali and Anaukaq were active and respected hunters. In the 1980s, accompanied by some of their children and grandchildren, they traveled to the United States and were reunited with their American relatives.

FAMILY REUNION

Through most of the twentieth century the existence of the Inughuit families that Peary and Henson left behind in Greenland was not widely known. But Donald MacMillan, who had met them on the 1908–1909 expedition, continued to work in the area, and he routinely visited and worked with them, although we do not know whether he reported back to the absent fathers. He did take photographs of the young men at different ages as they grew to be respected hunters in their community.

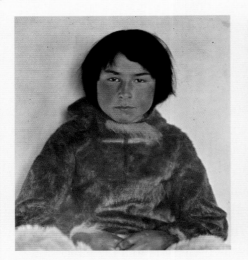 

Figures 95 and 96   Samik Peary in 1909 and 1924.

Figures 97 and 98   Kali Peary ca. 1914 and in 1954.

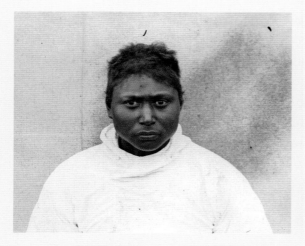

Figures 99 and 100   Anaukaq Henson in 1924 and 1938.

The American Peary family was aware of their relatives in Greenland but, out of deference to Josephine and Marie, made no attempts to contact them and never spoke of them publicly, although Jean Malaurie had written about them in the 1950s and John Weems mentioned their existence in his 1967 biography, *Peary, the Explorer and the Man*. Henson's nieces and nephews, however, did not know of his Inughuit son.

This situation changed in the 1980s, when explorer Wally Herbert and researcher S. Allen Counter separately learned of the families and worked to bring them together. Edward Stafford, Peary's oldest grandson, traveled to Greenland in 1988 to meet Kali and his son, as well as Samik's descendants. In 1988, representatives of both the Peary and the Henson families, as well as Odaq's son Iggianguaq, traveled to the United States to visit with their American relatives.

As is to be expected, the Inughuit did not forget Peary. Historian Kenn Harper spoke with some of them and their children when he lived in Qaanaaq in the 1980s, and while some, such as Odaq, recalled Peary fondly, others were less complimentary and remembered being afraid of him and of the repercussions of refusing him when he asked for something. Peary left a lasting impact on the community, but ultimately it was other factors that led to the greatest societal changes. With the establishment of the first mission station in 1909, and the Thule trading station in 1910, sustained change began to creep into Inughuit society. Over the years, as more services became available around the trading station, including a medical station and school, more and more families gathered there. In 1953, when the United States planned to expand use of the area around the Thule Air Base, constructed in 1951, the Inughuit families were forcibly displaced and moved to Qaanaaq, which has become the social, political, and economic hub of the region. Today, hunting continues to be important, and the Inughuit are still regarded as exceptional hunters by other Greenlanders as well as outsiders. But hunting is becoming an increasingly difficult way to make a living as global warming brings unprecedented changes to the region.

6

THE NORTH POLE
CONTROVERSY IN
HISTORICAL PERSPECTIVE

Who reached the North Pole first? Was it Frederick A. Cook in 1908 or Robert E. Peary in 1909? Was it Matthew Henson, who in 1909 walked ahead of Peary and thus likely reached the North Pole first? Or was it Ralph Plaisted, who got there in 1968? The North Pole controversy has a life and history of its own, developed over more than a century. Every 25 years since 1909 there has been a flurry of North Pole–related activity and publications, but the issues upon which people have focused have shifted over time, reflecting the Peary and Cook families' activities, societal developments, and national and international considerations.

A Controversy Is Born

On July 3, 1907, the schooner *John R. Bradley* left Gloucester, Massachusetts, and headed north, first to Nova Scotia, and then to Greenland. On board were passengers John R. Bradley, a wealthy sportsman and owner of the vessel, and Frederick A. Cook, an American physician and polar explorer. Cargo included supplies for Cook, who planned to winter in northwestern Greenland and attempt to reach the North Pole the following spring. In his 1911 book, *My Attainment of the Pole*, Cook wrote that an "Arctic expedition had been born without the usual clamor. Prepared in one month . . . no press heralded our project, no government aid had been asked, nor had large contributions been sought from private individuals." Cook accurately described his expedition, drawing not-so-subtle

Figure 101 Frederick A. Cook. Frederick Cook had no photographs of himself on his North Pole sledge journey, so he posed for this studio portrait, taken in New York in 1911. Some of the clothing he is wearing may be from his expedition, although the felt socks would not have been sufficient protection against the Arctic ice.

comparisons to Robert E. Peary's multiple North Pole efforts, which were planned for months (if not years), widely covered by the press, and funded by prominent, wealthy individuals and the Peary Arctic Club.

Neither Cook nor Bradley had mentioned Cook's intentions when the vessel left the United States. However, in letters from Etah, dated August 26, 1907—one addressed to Herbert Bridgman, secretary of the Peary Arctic Club, and the other to Henry C. Walsh, secretary of the Explorers Club—Cook made his intentions clear. Once Bradley was back in Nova Scotia, he mailed Cook's letters, which reached their intended recipients in early October, quickly becoming the subject of newspaper articles. Cook's letter to Bridgman read in part:

I have hit upon a new route to the North Pole and will stay to try it. By way of Buchanan Bay and Ellesmere Land and northward through Nansen Strait over the Polar sea [*sic*] seems to me to be a very good route. There will be game to the 82°, and here are natives and dogs for the task. So here is for the Pole. Mr. Bradley will tell you the rest. Kind regards to all—F. A. Cook

The *Roosevelt*, back from Peary's failed 1905–1906 North Pole expedition, was undergoing repairs in 1907 when the *Bradley* sailed north. Peary had hoped to depart for another attempt to reach the North Pole that summer, but, due to funding and refitting delays, the *Roosevelt* was not ready. Peary knew he would have to wait until 1908 to launch another expedition to reach the North Pole and was incensed when he heard about Cook's plans. He believed that Cook had unethically encroached on his territory and his relationship with the people of northwestern Greenland. The North Pole controversy was taking shape.

Fears Confirmed

On July 6, 1908, the *Roosevelt* sailed north, reaching northwestern Greenland in early August. There, Peary learned that Cook had departed on his North Pole journey with two Inughuit, Ittukusuk and Aapilaq, having left Rudolph Franke, a *Bradley* crew member, living in a house Cook had built at Anoritok. Franke was not in good physical or mental shape and returned to the United States on Peary's relief ship, having signed over responsibility for Cook's belongings to Peary. Peary took over the house, installing two *Roosevelt* crewmen in it, as well as Harry Whitney, the wealthy big-game hunter who planned to spend the 1908–1909 winter hunting in the Arctic.

In August 1909, after Peary returned from the North Pole and the *Roosevelt* left its Cape Sheridan anchorage, the vessel reached northwestern Greenland, where it dropped off the Inughuit families that had worked with Peary. There Peary and his men learned that Cook had returned to his house after wintering at Cape Sparbo on Devon Island. Cook had subsequently proceeded south by dog sledge to catch a ship bound for Europe. Then Peary's party learned that Cook claimed to have reached the North Pole. Chief Engineer George Wardwell's August 25, 1909, journal entry reports, "Dr. Cook sent word by the whaler at Upernivik [*sic*] that he got the pole the 20th of last April." Wardwell's entry for that day continued, referring to what Peary's men had learned from questioning Ittukusuk and Aapilaq: "And the two Eskimos he had with him said he only left the land for two days and went back South [*sic*] to Jone's [*sic*] Sound, he claimed to [have] found new land but the Eskimos

Figure 102   Ittukusuk and Aapilaq with Cook's Sledge. Once they had lost all of their dogs, Ittukusuk and Aapilaq hauled Cook's light sledge by hand. Eventually they abandoned it, too. Nevertheless, the three men completed an epic sledge journey, returning safely to Anoritok after more than a year of travel.

say they didnt [*sic*] see any. And they can see about as far as anybody." Peary's fears that Cook would try to rob him of the North Pole prize were confirmed.

Conflicting North Pole Claims

On September 1, 1909, Cook, not a widely recognized public personality, cabled the startling news to the *New York Herald* from the telegraph station in Lerwick, Shetland Islands, that he had reached the North Pole on April 21, 1908. The Lerwick wireless station was the first one he could reach while sailing from southern Greenland to Copenhagen on the *Hans Egede*. In the following days, the front pages of newspapers throughout Europe and the United States carried the astonishing news, recapped the long history of explorers trying to reach the North Pole, and published interviews with prominent individuals who expressed varying opinions about the believability of Cook's announcement. Cook arrived in Copenhagen on September 4, where hundreds of people waited to greet him. The newspaper coverage intensified as reporters interviewed him and arrangements to honor him were formalized.

On September 6, two days after Cook reached Copenhagen, Peary reached Indian Harbour, the northernmost wireless station in southern

Labrador, and sent messages announcing that he had reached the North Pole on April 6, 1909. On September 7, the *New York Times*, which had exclusive rights to Peary's story, devoted the first four and a half pages of the paper to North Pole developments. The newspaper described him as "the hero of eight polar expeditions, covering a period of twenty-three years," and emphasized his status as a well-known, respected, and seasoned explorer (with the contrast to Cook implied). As Peary's announcement spread around the world, Cook was in Europe being celebrated as the first man to have reached the North Pole.

On September 7, 1909, articles appeared in various newspapers reporting that Peary, who was still in southern Labrador, declared that he, not Cook, was the first person to reach the North Pole. According to a *Boston Globe* article, Peary claimed that Cook could not have carried enough supplies to accomplish the task and that he purposely traveled to unexplored regions of the Arctic, where his activities could not be documented.

The following day, the *New York Times* published an article titled "Dr. Cook Gets Gold Medal," describing the contents of a lecture Cook had delivered. The article reported that Cook acknowledged that his success was built on the work of others, mentioning Fridtjof Nansen and Peary in

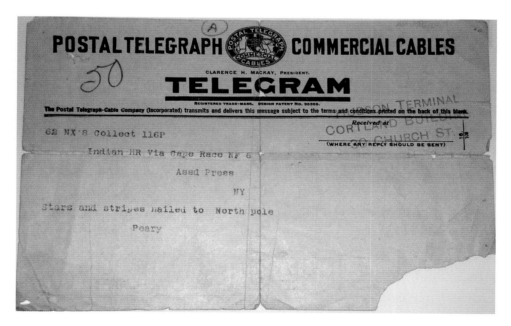

Figure 103   Telegram Sent from Labrador. Peary sent brief telegrams to his family, important backers, and key news outlets from Indian Harbour, Labrador, which had a small wireless relay station connecting it to Battle Harbour, where the main station was located. The wording clearly positioned him as a successful and patriotic achiever.

particular. Cook saved his greatest appreciation for Otto Sverdrup, whose 1898–1902 expedition narrative helped Cook determine from what point of land he would approach the Pole. Cook's mention of Sverdrup would have been particularly galling to Peary, who considered Sverdrup a North Pole rival.

Herbert L. Bridgman, one of the individuals to whom Cook had sent his 1907 North Pole message and an ardent Peary supporter, wrote an article that appeared in the September 9, 1909, weekly publication *The Independent*. Titled "Dash to the Pole," it was written with the intention of diminishing Cook's standing by downplaying his credentials as an explorer and questioning whether his expedition had any scientific value, while detailing the scientific contributions made by other polar explorers, including Peary. Bridgman pointedly questioned Cook's ethics and sense of fair play:

Maybe this is not the time nor place to intrude ethics or etiquet [*sic*]. Yet those who have followed Arctic matters do not forget that Peary made all this possible, and they reserve until the facts are known their judgment. Eskimos had been trained by him, lands explored and seas charted, and only an unlucky delay of contractors, for which he was in no way responsible, kept him at home in the summer of 1907.

Bridgman went on to complain about the secrecy surrounding Cook's departure, noting that Cook knew full well that Peary was going to make another attempt to reach the North Pole. Bridgman charged that Cook had robbed Peary of the opportunity to complete his work while benefiting from what Peary had learned.

The September 9 edition of the *New York Times* was again full of North Pole–related news. The most important piece was a message from Peary printed on the front page with an Indian Harbour, September 8 dateline. It read, "Cook's story should not be taken too seriously. The Eskimos who accompanied him say he went no distance north. He did not get out of sight of land." A message sent by Peary to his wife was quoted in the same article: "Don't let Cook story worry you. Have him nailed."

The second page of the newspaper was full of North Pole stories as well. One was by Cyrus C. Adams, a journalist turned geographer who had described some of Peary's earlier Greenland ice cap work. Adams characterized Peary as remarkable. He calculated Peary's sledging speeds, noting that they were the fastest recorded by explorers. He observed that not only Peary but also some of his assistants had achieved farthest north records that superseded those of accomplished and respected explorers. He attributed these accomplishments to Peary's focus on the art of sledging. He concluded the article by stating that Peary's accomplishment was the result of years of experience:

> The conquest of the pole was not the work merely of last March and April. Every year that Peary has been in the field he has learned something new that counted in the great cumulation. . . . So it has gone from year to year till now, when the quintessence of experience and the qualities of the masterful explorer have united to reveal the pole and put an end to the quest of centuries.

Another article appearing in the September 9 issue reported that Peary's cable challenging Cook's account concerned a number of people. Bradley was quoted as observing that both men needed to provide proof of their accomplishments. He also responded to Peary's statement that the two Inughuit who had accompanied Cook had not corroborated his account of the North Pole journey by questioning whether the word and observations of the Inughuit, referred to as Eskimos, could be trusted.

Peary's announcement and early accounts came under intense scrutiny and criticism as well. A September 11, 1909, story on the front page of the *Boston Daily Globe* noted that Peary's account was quite similar to Cook's both in terms of ice conditions described and in terminology used. The author of the article concluded that this similarity lent support to Cook's claim to have been the first person to reach the North Pole. Also, the travel speeds the men achieved on given days were compared. Peary's rapid sledging speeds would come under more scrutiny in the following days.

Then the article focused on who Peary chose to take to the Pole, noting, "He chose to part with his last white companion and make the dash to the pole with only his negro [sic] servant, Matthew Henson, and Eskimos." Why had Peary not taken another white man with him? This question would become the focus of future critiques. The article concluded by criticizing both Peary and Cook for lack of detail in their descriptions and the absence of a corroborating white witness.

Now at Battle Harbour, which had an excellent anchorage, facilities, and a wireless station, Peary faced the fact that Cook, rather than he, was being

Figure 104   Peary at Battle Harbour. This is a rare image of Peary smiling, taken at Battle Harbour before the controversy had gotten really ugly. It suggests Peary's initial confidence that his reputation and experience would outweigh Cook's claims.

honored as the man who had first reached the North Pole. His fury grew. He sent a wireless message on September 10, which was published on the front page of the *New York Times* the following day: "Do not trouble about Cook's story or attempt to explain any discrepancies in his statements. The affair will settle itself. He has not been at the pole on April 21st, 1908, or at any other time. He has simply handed the public a gold brick." This hostile and disparaging characterization of Cook garnered Peary few fans and troubled Peary's backers, including Thomas Hubbard, who began to counsel Peary about what he should and should not say publicly.

Beau Riffenburgh, who has documented the role that the press played in the North Pole controversy, pointed out that the press further sensationalized the claims because newspapers were experiencing a brisk business, and the general public was totally caught up in the controversy. Cartoonists chimed in as well, having fun depicting various facets of the conflict. Merchandisers also saw a market in the controversy, producing a number of North Pole–themed items that they sold to the public.

Figure 105–107   North Pole Merchandise. It was not only newspapers that saw an opportunity to make money from the controversy. People were eager to purchase all manner of goods, often to express their opinion about who had been at the North Pole. The United States Tobacco Company put its money on Peary, who endorsed "North Pole Smoking Tobacco." People could purchase a ceramic mug in the form of Peary or, if they were on the fence, a lapel tag proclaiming their support of Peary on one side and Cook on the other.

Figure 108 *Le Petit Journal.* The North Pole controversy was not confined to the United States. European newspapers were also eager to enter the fray. *Le Petit Journal* in Paris developed this dramatic and entertaining cover, complete with a ring of skeptical Antarctic penguins observing the battle between Cook and Peary.

Things Get Nastier

In late September, the wireless at Indian Harbour hummed again, this time with word from Harry Whitney, the big-game hunter who had spent the 1908–1909 winter in northwestern Greenland. When Cook returned to Anoritok after his North Pole trip, he was a guest in his own house, now inhabited by Peary's men and Whitney. Whitney treated Cook with kindness, and Cook came to trust him. Cook was determined to get to Copenhagen that fall and faced an arduous journey south to intercept a Europe-bound vessel. He entrusted Whitney with his instruments and many of his papers, believing that he could not safely take them with him. Cook expected that Whitney would return his belongings once both men were back in the United States. In the late September wireless messages, however, Whitney reported that he did not have Cook's papers and instruments with him.

Whitney had expected that the vessel he had hired, the *Jeanie*, would pick him up during the summer of 1909, but in late August, as the *Roosevelt* prepared to leave northwestern Greenland, the *Jeanie* had not arrived. Peary offered to take him south on the *Roosevelt* but prohibited him from placing any of Cook's belongings on board the ship. Whitney left them in a rock cache at Etah. The *Roosevelt* and the *Jeanie* met up a day's sail from Etah, and Whitney transferred ships. The *Jeanie* remained in the Arctic so Whitney could do some more hunting, but Whitney decided not to return to Etah to retrieve Cook's belongings.

Cook, a mild-mannered and unassuming man, was devastated. Without his instruments and papers, he could not produce the documentation that geographic societies were demanding. Upon hearing the story about Peary barring Whitney from transporting Cook's belongings south, people lost respect and sympathy for Peary. He had become increasingly shrill in his demands that his rival provide proof of his accomplishments. Yet, people pointed out, Peary had made sure that Cook did not have access to the very papers and instruments Peary was demanding that Cook produce.

The initial North Pole accounts provided by both explorers were judged to have significant problems. Both were vague in places, did not contain the kind of information that expert scientists and armchair explorers expected, and different versions of each man's account were not always consistent. Suggestions that both men submit documentation of their claims to an independent board went nowhere. Cook had minimal documentation, and Peary refused to open his records to scrutiny. As Lyle Dick has nicely documented, while Cook was left to defend himself, Peary had the backing of influential members of the Peary Arctic Club, who tried to manage what Peary said publicly while actively discrediting Cook by raising questions about some of his past accomplishments.

Major Issues in the Early 1900s

Over the next two years, the pros and cons of the two explorers' claims were rehashed endlessly. The major issues revolved around race, technological feasibility, navigation, photographic evidence, similarities of the narratives, and personal character.

Race

Why Peary sent Bartlett, captain of the *Roosevelt* and an excellent navigator, back to the ship and took Matthew Henson and four Inughuit with him on the last leg of the journey to the North Pole was discussed at length.

At the time, African Americans were rarely respected, indigenous people were seen as backward, and neither group was seen as providing credible witnesses. Peary offered various reasons as to why he chose to have Henson and not Bartlett with him, but his explanations did not satisfy people. Similarly, Cook was faulted for not including another white person on his expedition. The individual talents of the explorers' Inughuit companions were neither discussed nor appreciated.

Henson embarked on a lecture tour shortly after returning to the United States and in 1912 published *A Negro Explorer at the North Pole*, with an introduction by Peary. As Emma Bonanomi has noted, the public and press attending Henson's lectures were quite torn about how to view him. He was an African American, so people were prepared to taunt and heckle him; yet some of those who went to hear him were struck by his knowledge and experience.

Navigation Methods, Readings, and Traveling Speeds

Peary's methods of navigation were questioned because he did not take longitudinal readings that people believed would have allowed him to account for the southeastward drift of the ice. Also, there were days when he did not take any readings at all. Cook, who was an inexperienced navigator and needed to practice using a sextant on his way to Greenland, had few documents to offer beyond his narratives and some summaries he had prepared when he was still in possession of his original records.

Could Cook have made the journey solely using the supplies carried by his party? People doubted it. Unlike Peary, he would not have been able to rely on caches of supplies strategically placed along his route.

If Cook and Peary were to be believed, both explorers made excellent time when distances they covered were compared with sledging records of other explorers. Peary's sledging speeds exceeded Cook's, and he reported his fastest sledging speeds after Bartlett turned back, arousing additional skepticism.

Photographs

Photographs reportedly taken when Cook and Peary were at the North Pole were scrutinized. Interestingly, neither man appears in any of the photographs, despite the fact that there is ample evidence that Inughuit traveling with MacMillan and Borup took photographs using the Americans' cameras.

Figure 109 Cook's North Pole Camp. Ittukusuk and Aapilaq stand by an igloo with a large American flag, with a sledge and some gear nearby. Cook took a number of images at this spot, ultimately the only evidence of his location.

Figure 110 Peary's North Pole Camp. Peary photographed the activities around the North Pole camp, complete with boots drying on snowshoes standing in the snow. He also photographed the North Pole flag from different angles, and with and without the other men standing by.

People studied the positions and lengths of shadows in the explorers' photographs. Thomas F. Hall, in his 1917 book, *Has the North Pole Been Discovered?*, criticized the positions of shadows in Peary's North Pole photographs and questioned whether they were all taken on the same day. He went on to focus on the shadows evident in a photograph Cook published titled "Mending Near the Pole" and claimed, "If the latitude where the picture was taken had been given, and that latitude was near the Pole, it would under the circumstances be the best evidence yet produced that Cook was at the Pole."

Similarity of the Men's Accounts

People were struck by the similarities in the preliminary accounts produced by Cook and Peary. If both men had reached the North Pole, the agreement between the accounts suggested that Cook had reached the Pole before Peary. Hall, in an extended critique of Peary, went so far as to raise the possibility of plagiarism.

Personal Character

People came to understand that there was no way to independently verify the competing claims, so they assessed the credibility of each man. Individuals like Hall, while purporting to judge the men on facts only, wrote, "Nothing in Cook's narrative, at first reading, seriously aroused my suspicions, as did the narrative of Peary." Hall could find no "ulterior motive" for Cook to fake his claim. Peary's supporters cited his experience and character, asserting that if he said he had been to the Pole, he was to be believed. They raised concerns about Cook's character given his claim of having climbed Mount McKinley, which they said was now disputed.

The North Pole controversy was not resolved, but Peary's supporters advanced his claim and secured him a congressional hearing in hopes that he would be declared the discoverer of the North Pole. The congressmen in the January 1911 hearing were frustrated with Peary, whom they found evasive. He felt abused by them. Nevertheless, in early March, by a narrow margin, a bill was passed, and it was signed by President William Howard Taft. It credited Peary with reaching the North Pole—though it did not declare him the man who "discovered" the North Pole. He and his white assistants were showered with praise, and he was honored throughout the world. Some African American groups honored Henson, who was

Figure 111   Canadian Camp Celebratory Banquet. Peary and Cook were each celebrated at numerous banquets. This is the cover of a menu for a banquet hosted in Peary's honor by the Canadian Camp, a club of influential sportsmen from the United States and Canada. They were known for serving exotic foods, and this meal included hardtack biscuits from the *Roosevelt*'s stores, as well as coffee made from 30-year-old beans brought back from Greely's supplies at Fort Conger.

otherwise denied the recognition given to his less accomplished white companions. The individual Inughuit did not factor into the celebrations at all.

The Twenty-Fifth Anniversary

In the early 1930s, the controversy over who first reached the North Pole was very much alive. Peary had died in 1920. In May 1926, within days of one another, Roald Amundsen, Umberto Nobile, and Lincoln Ellsworth (flying aboard the airship *Norge*) and Richard Byrd and Floyd Bennett (flying a Fokker tri-motor airplane, the *Josephine Ford*) flew over the North Pole. Cook, who in 1923 had been convicted of fraud and incarcerated over a different issue, had been pardoned by President Calvin Coolidge and left prison in March 1930. Henson, Bartlett, and MacMillan were all alive, as was Peary's wife Josephine, though her daughter, Marie Peary Stafford, was the family spokesperson.

As the twenty-fifth anniversary of the discovery of the North Pole approached, concern about defending Peary's claim was a topic of conversation among those who believed in him. Hall's 1917 book, critiquing Peary for nearly 350 pages, was of particular concern. Peary's supporters faced the problem of explaining errors, inconsistencies, and gaps in Peary's various narratives.

To make matters worse, in 1929, J. Gordon Hayes wrote an entire book critical of Peary, titled *Robert Edwin Peary: A Record of His Explorations 1886–1909*. Hayes, a cleric who had never been to the Arctic, concluded that Peary had failed to reach the North Pole. He charged that while Peary did discover new land, he failed to collect valuable scientific information about it or survey it accurately. He accused Peary of not choosing companions who were fully qualified, instead using "Henson and the Eskimos as his companions, in spite of the fact that all of them, from the most important standpoints, were perfectly useless."

On the second page of the preface, in a statement dated September 21, 1929, Hayes announced that he had been contacted by an individual who wanted to remain anonymous and who claimed to have been Peary's amanuensis and to have written 80 percent of *The North Pole* book. Hayes wrote that it would "take time to clear everything up. That Peary inscribed a deliberate lie on his title-page is simply incredible."

People were aware that Hayes was publishing another book about Arctic exploration that would contain a chapter critical of Peary. Vilhjalmur Stefansson, a well-known Arctic explorer, wanted to refute Hayes's charges. Stefansson had been collecting letters from men who participated on the expedition as well as from people like Peter Freuchen, who worked and lived among Inughuit and had discussed the two expeditions with them. MacMillan, now a well-known explorer, was busy as well, corresponding with fellow expedition members about how to handle the upcoming North Pole anniversary.

Marie Peary Stafford had strong opinions about how the twenty-fifth anniversary should be handled and made it clear that she did not want any of the explorers to serve as spokesmen for her family. She was particularly sensitive about revelations that ghostwriters had helped Peary write descriptions of his expedition that had appeared in *Hampton's Magazine* and *The North Pole*, believing this information would reflect badly on her father, despite the fact that ghostwriting was not unusual at the time.

Meanwhile, some were attempting to get Henson's significant contributions to the expedition recognized. Morgan State University and Howard

Figure 112 Marie Peary Stafford. Marie Peary Stafford nurtured her father's legacy throughout her life. Here she stands with Donald MacMillan aboard the USS *Peary*, which was set to carry amphibious planes to Etah, Greenland, so MacMillan and Richard Byrd could test them for a possible flight over the North Pole.

University awarded him honorary degrees in 1924 and 1939, respectively, and he was admitted into the Explorers Club in 1937 thanks to the efforts of fellow explorers MacMillan and Stefansson.

In anticipation of the twenty-fifth anniversary, a flurry of North Pole–focused publications appeared. MacMillan published *How Peary Reached the Pole* in 1934. In this book, he spelled out Peary's attention to detail and the methods Peary had employed to ensure that the men were prepared for their arduous work. Also, he reported that in 1913 he had had the opportunity to travel and speak with Ittukusuk. They visited Cook's camps on Axel Heiberg Island, and Ittukusuk confirmed that Cook had not gone near the North Pole.

Hayes's *The Conquest of the North Pole*, with its negative chapter about Peary, appeared in 1934, despite efforts by Peary supporters to delay its publication. Hayes elaborated on his earlier ghostwriter accusation, this time naming the ghostwriter. He reported that Peary "supplied Mr. A. E. Thomas with the subject-matter from which Mr. Thomas wrote the book, though his name does not appear and his authorship is a secret."

Jeannette Mirsky's classic, *To the Arctic! The Story of Northern Exploration from Earliest Times*, was also released in 1934. She supported Peary's claim and did not believe Cook's, citing, among other things, testimony given by a number of Danes working among the Inughuit that Cook's account was not corroborated by his Inughuit companions. Mirsky and her publisher were sued by Cook for defamation of character. Correspondence in MacMillan's papers at Bowdoin College suggests that Cook moved to sue MacMillan as well.

Walter Henry Lewin came out with *The Great North Pole Fraud* in 1935, which was critical of Peary, and William Herbert Hobbs published *Peary*, a sympathetic biography in 1936. Hobbs had known Peary, consulted with Bartlett and MacMillan, and in the book thanked Marie Peary Stafford for her assistance. He concluded the account of Peary's Arctic career with a quote from the *Nation* that stated in part, "As for Peary himself he has been defrauded of something which can never be restored to him . . . the joy of the acclaim that should have greeted him at this triumphant close of his twenty-three years [*sic*] quest can never be his."

In response to the anniversary, and despite Marie's wishes, Henson, Freuchen, Bartlett, MacMillan, and others spoke out in Peary's defense, and MacMillan produced a 15-page point-by-point refutation of Hayes's charges. Most of the major issues that emerged between 1909 and 1911 were rehashed. There was some discussion about flying Ittukusuk and Aapilaq to the United States to testify, but that never happened.

The new development was the now common knowledge that ghost-writers had helped Peary write the piece in *Hampton's Magazine* (Elsa Barker) and *The North Pole* (A. E. Thomas). Cook had employed a ghost-writer (T. Everett Harré) as well. As Lyle Dick, Michael Robinson, and Robert Bryce have pointed out, the knowledge that both men employed ghostwriters only complicated critiques of the explorers. Who was responsible for the errors and inconsistencies in the explorers' accounts? Who was responsible for what some people saw as the striking similarities of the narratives?

The Fiftieth Anniversary

By the 1950s, the United States and the Soviet Union were engaged in the Cold War. Both countries saw space as the new frontier and trained men to be astronauts, the new explorers of the mid-twentieth century. The territory of Alaska became the forty-ninth U.S. state in 1959, further establishing the country's identity as an Arctic nation, and a dozen countries signed the Antarctic Treaty, which designated the Antarctic as a preserve in which scientific investigations, but not military activities, could take place.

In the late 1940s, Matthew Henson received recognition in corridors previously closed to him. In 1947, Bradley Robinson published a biography of Henson titled *Dark Companion*, with an introduction by Donald MacMillan. The following year, due to the efforts of MacMillan and Zenith Radio founder Eugene McDonald, Henson received a gold medal from the Geographical Society of Chicago, with the presentation broadcast over radio. Henson and his wife Lucy were invited to the White House in 1954, where he was recognized for his achievements by President Dwight D. Eisenhower. Henson remained a well-liked and respected visitor to the Explorers Club until his death in 1955.

In 1955, Helene Cook Vetter, Frederick Cook's daughter, published *Return from the Pole*, which had been handwritten by her father in the 1930s. The introduction by Frederick J. Pohl was part biography of Cook, part review of the chronology of the original controversy, and part exposé of the Peary campaign to discredit Cook. He concluded his piece arguing that, like Columbus, Cook was a great explorer who had suffered great injustice.

In 1960, John E. Weems, who, with the benefit of access to Peary family papers, would go on to publish a flattering biography of Peary, published *Race for the Pole*. The preface, written by Stefansson, was a fresh attack on Cook's claim and character. Weems's pro-Peary stance is clear throughout the volume not only in how he depicts the two explorers but also in how he characterizes their wives. Attitudes about the two explorers remained polarized, and critiques remained deeply personal.

As the fiftieth anniversary of the North Pole controversy approached, MacMillan, 88 and now an admiral, was the only surviving member of Peary's North Pole expedition, for Odaq had died in 1955. MacMillan and his schooner *Bowdoin*, which he had had custom built for Arctic work, were in the news as the vessel took what people imagined would be its last voyage to Mystic, Connecticut, to become part of a maritime museum exhibition.

The North Pole was again in the news in 1958, as the submarine USS *Nautilus* transited the Northwest Passage and crossed the North Pole while submerged, and in 1959, when the USS *Skate* became the first American submarine to surface at the North Pole. Those voyages

Figure 113 USS *Skate* at the North Pole. In 1958, the nuclear submarine USS *Skate* was the second submarine to go to the North Pole, after the USS *Nautilus*. The ice at the Pole was too thick to break through that year, but the *Skate* returned in 1959 and was able to break through the ice, the first submarine ever to do so.

demonstrated the United States' strength and its sovereignty claims, while also sending a message that the United States considered the Northwest Passage an international waterway.

In commemoration of the fiftieth anniversary of Peary's North Pole expedition, the United States Postal Service issued a 4-cent stamp featuring a faint circumpolar map. Against it, Peary, dressed in furs, was depicted dog sledging over the ice-covered Polar Sea. In juxtaposition to the man-dog endeavor was the nuclear submarine *Nautilus* transiting the Arctic Ocean under the ice, a symbol of United States' power and advanced technological prowess.

Addressing the Cook-Peary controversy more directly, John Euller published a negative article about Peary that was largely a restatement of the Hill and Hayes positions. MacMillan's copy, housed at Bowdoin College, includes a typed comment by MacMillan or his wife Miriam that reads, "Aren't any of our Great Men safe from defamation after death?"

The Seventy-Fifth Anniversary

Whereas the fiftieth anniversary of the controversy was relatively subdued, the seventy-fifth anniversary had significant prominence. In 1968,

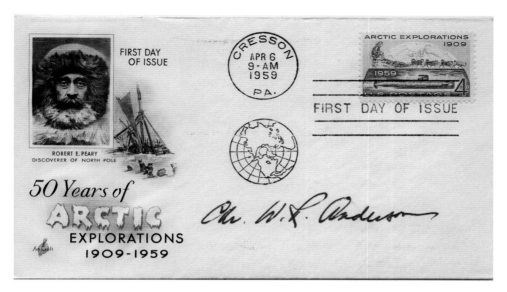

Figure 114 Fiftieth Anniversary Stamp. The U.S. Postal Service marked the fiftieth anniversary of Peary's trip to the Pole, and the USS *Nautilus* becoming the first submarine to reach the Pole, with a commemorative stamp. This first day cover, issued on April 6, 1959, from the post office in Peary's birthplace, Cresson, Pennsylvania, is signed by Commander William R. Anderson, who commanded the *Nautilus* on that historic voyage.

Ralph Plaisted, an insurance man who became enamored with snowmobiles, along with Gerald Pitzl, Jean-Luc Bombardier, and Walter Pederson, reached the North Pole using Bombardier snowmobiles on April 19. U.S. and Canadian flags were planted at the Pole, and the party's position was verified by a U.S. Air Force plane. Here, then, was the independent verification missing from all earlier North Pole claims.

On April 6, 1969, Wally Herbert, with a team of three other men and forty dogs, reached the North Pole, having sledged from Point Barrow, Alaska. The feat was accomplished again in May 1971 by Inughuit descendants of Peary and Henson, who were supporting the Italian North Pole Expedition, and repeated in 1978 by a Japanese expedition. In 1986, Will Steger and Paul Schurke led a dog-sledging expedition to the North Pole, following Peary's route as closely as possible. Ann Bancroft, the first woman to reach the North Pole, was a member of the Steger-Schurke team. The top of the world was no longer the purview of men only.

In 1973, another book attacking Peary's character and record was published, this one by Dennis Rawlins, under the title *Peary at the North Pole: Fact or Fiction?* That same year, Hugh Eames published *Winner Lose All: Dr. Cook and the Theft of the North Pole.* In 1983, a docudrama,

Cook & Peary: The Race to the Pole, aired on television, starring Richard Chamberlain as Frederick Cook. The program was sympathetic to Cook and characterized Peary in unflattering ways.

Robert Peary's family had donated all of his papers to the National Archives and Records Administration in the 1960s with the stipulation that some of the admiral's papers, including his 1909 North Pole journal, would remain closed to the public. The journal was reclassified in 1986. Cook's records had remained in his family's hands. Upon the death of Cook's granddaughter Janet Vetter in 1984, his papers were donated to the Library of Congress.

In anticipation of the seventy-fifth anniversary of the North Pole controversy, people combed through the two explorers' newly accessible records, seeking that elusive evidence they thought would prove or disprove each man's claim. The characters of Cook and Peary remained the focus of attention, and neither man escaped scathing critiques.

The analyses of experts were plagued by apparent conflicts of interest. For instance, Wally Herbert concluded that neither Cook nor Peary had reached the North Pole. If that were true, Herbert would be the first person to dog sledge to the North Pole. The Foundation for the Promotion of the Art of Navigation was asked by the National Geographic Society to examine all the navigation issues associated with Peary's claim. Among the new analytical techniques that they used was forensic photography, last attempted in a rudimentary way by Hall in his 1917 publication. They concluded that on April 6 and 7, 1909, Peary was "within four or five miles of his reported position and certainly not more than fifteen miles away." While some people find this report credible, critics point to the self-interest of the National Geographic Society, as that organization had been and remained a key supporter of Peary's claim.

Matthew Henson's role in the North Pole controversy changed dramatically around this anniversary, in light of the civil rights movement and largely through the efforts of S. Allen Counter, a physician who became interested in Henson, having met some of his Inughuit relatives. Henson was declared co-discoverer of the North Pole, and he was reburied, along with his wife, next to Peary at Arlington National Cemetery. Also, in 1986, the United States issued a polar explorer stamp series, including a 22-cent U.S. stamp featuring portraits of Peary and Henson. At various times in his life Henson had reported that he had walked ahead of Peary, likely reaching the North Pole first. This account was promoted, with Henson supporters declaring that he, rather than Peary, was the first person to stand at the North Pole.

The other shift in focus at this time involved the Inughuit. The various Inughuit descendants of Peary and Henson, and of Inughuit who had been on the final leg of the North Pole trip, visited the United States. Counter flew members of the Peary and Henson families to the United States, where they met some of their American relatives. Bowdoin College sponsored a reunion of members of Peary's family, along with Odaq's descendants. Stories about these multiracial, multicultural families were featured in the press. Some stories sensationalized the fact that Peary and Henson had had Inughuit wives, while other stories reported on the excitement family members felt as they met relatives from another culture.

The Hundredth Anniversary

By 2009, the North Pole was a tourist destination and a place to conduct scientific work, as well as a place for adventure. Some people, like Tom Avery, a mountaineer and polar adventurer, tried to re-create Peary's 1908–1909 North Pole journey using dogs and wooden sledges. His 2005 team, led by experienced dog-sledge driver Matty McNair, made record time, and he argued that his expedition demonstrated that Peary reached the North Pole as he had claimed. Others traveled to the Pole on icebreakers, planes, and helicopters. The North Pole Environmental Observatory was established in 2000 using new technologies that allowed scientists to remotely collect environmental data throughout the year. A webcam was set up as part of the project, and for the next 14 years people around the world could view the ice conditions at the Pole while sitting at their desks.

At the same time, the Arctic Ocean was experiencing a decline in sea ice, and questions surfaced regarding control of this body of water. In August 2007, Russia sent two mini-submarines to the ocean floor and placed a titanium Russian flag on the seabed at the North Pole. The century-old controversy over which of two Americans had discovered the North Pole was not discussed. When the Russians planted their flag, they were focused on the Lomonosov Ridge, an underwater mountain ridge that extends from Ellesmere Island, passes near the North Pole, and continues to a point near the New Siberian Islands.

The multi-year ice over which past explorers toiled was rapidly disappearing. The prospect of a largely ice-free Arctic Ocean concerned

Figure 115 North Pole Webcam. Each spring between 2002 and 2015 National Oceanic and Atmospheric Administration and Pacific Marine Environmental Laboratory scientists working near the North Pole set up webcams as part of a long-term project to study the environment. The webcams transmitted multiple images a day via satellite for as long as there was daylight, from April to October. Because they were set up on the sea ice, the webcams did not stay at the North Pole; their location as the ice drifted was logged by GPS.

environmental scientists, environmental policymakers, and northern residents. At the same time, countries and organizations recognized the economic opportunities presented by a seasonally ice-free Arctic Ocean. The Russians were busy building a case for claiming a large segment of the ocean floor based on the geography off their continental shelf, as were the other nations that rim the Arctic Ocean. One hundred years ago, people were preoccupied with who first got to the North Pole and whether there was land at or near the Pole. In the early twenty-first century, the Arctic again preoccupied many nations, but it was not what land was on the ocean's surface, but rather what could be found under the ocean floor, that was of interest.

The North Pole controversy is still the subject of inquiry on the part of scholars. In 1997, Robert M. Bryce published a large volume titled *Cook & Peary: The Polar Controversy, Resolved,* but of course in many people's minds it has not been settled. However, the borderline obsession with judging the characters of Peary and Cook has been replaced by an interest in understanding the social, economic, political, and environmental context in which Arctic expeditions were launched and in which explorers operated. While people continue to read Cook's and Peary's papers, of equal interest are the papers and photographs of expedition members barely mentioned in the published North Pole narratives. Scholars have studied the financial and philosophical attitudes of Peary supporters, notions of manliness as exemplified by explorers, the significant and largely unacknowledged roles played by women associated with expeditions, and how international relations played out through various expeditions. The significant contributions of Inughuit and other Inuit to Arctic exploration have been examined, as have the negative effects of this colonial activity.

The North Pole, the point around which the world rotates, is a peculiar place. The moment someone reaches it they are south of it due to floating ice, ocean currents, and wind. It has a magical allure but is also maddeningly elusive, for while its location is clear conceptually, it is difficult to remain there physically. The North Pole controversy has taken on the characteristic of the Pole itself. Countless people thought they had found the key piece of evidence that would clarify who reached the North Pole first, but proof has remained elusive. And, like the North Pole, its elusiveness has proved to be its attraction.

We will never know for certain who reached the North Pole first, and it no longer matters. Rather, our challenge is to figure out how to peacefully and responsibly navigate the new environmental, social, economic, and political waters at the top of the world.

7

THE CONTEMPORARY ARCTIC

Today, more than 100 years after Cook and Peary ventured onto the Polar Sea, the Arctic is a profoundly different place. Where the land was once inhabited by small, mobile bands of indigenous groups, there are now settled communities, including cities in some parts of the Arctic. Where travel was once possible only by boat and dog sledge, airplanes and helicopters connect communities. Also, modern communications systems such as radios, mobile phones, and satellite phones allow people to stay in touch with each other and the rest of the world. Some of the most profound and noticeable changes that have come, however, are environmental. In particular, the reduction in the amount of ice covering the Polar Sea due to rapidly rising temperatures is impacting all aspects of life in the North. In what ways is the region that Peary and Cook explored different from what it was a century ago?

An Open Polar Sea?

During Peary and Cook's time, the Arctic Ocean was full of multi-year ice, ice that persisted in the Arctic Ocean over many years, growing thicker each winter. Expanses of it were the platforms on which Peary's men moved food and equipment north. As their descriptions make clear, however, this multi-year ice, sometimes more than 16 feet thick, was not stable. Rather, it was moved around by wind and currents, so it sometimes cracked open, forming leads of open water, and sometimes crashed together—vast floes rafting on top of each other and creating jagged, seemingly impassable barriers or pressure ridges.

Some of this multi-year ice was carried south and out of the Arctic Ocean by strong currents flowing through Nares Strait and Fram Strait.

Figure 116 Standing on a Pressure Ridge. Three of Peary's men stand atop a massive pressure ridge formed from thick multi-year ice. Such mountains of ice were a significant barrier to the men as they sledged north and required hours of difficult work to get across.

The Irminger Current swept pack ice down the east Greenland coast, around the southern end of Greenland, and counterclockwise into Davis Strait, where it (along with ice carried by the Baffin Current) created significant hazards for vessels plying Arctic waters. This was the ice that the *Roosevelt* rammed through before the pack became impenetrable north of Cape Sheridan. This was the ice that Wardwell listened for as he worried about the safety of the vessel.

Peary and other explorers working in the Arctic learned what Inuit already knew: that there was year-to-year variability in the development of new ice and the distribution of multi-year ice. In 1905–1906, for example, Peary's progress was repeatedly impeded by areas of open water. Explorers could meticulously plan for various contingencies, but their work was subject to natural disruptions they could not predict.

Today, large sections of the Arctic are warming, and the region is experiencing a significant reduction in sea ice. The extent of the Arctic

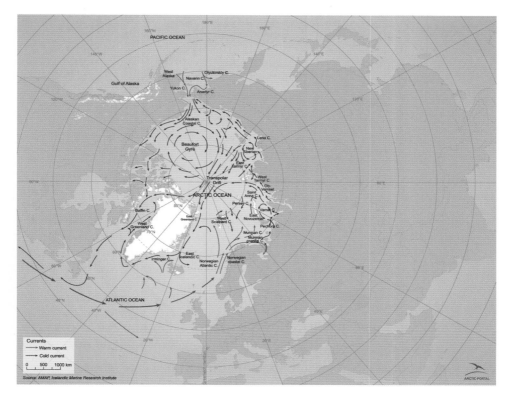

Figure 117   Arctic Currents. Currents in and around the Arctic Ocean move sea ice in complex ways. Ice caught in the Beaufort Gyre or in the small channels between the High Arctic Islands can survive for many years and grow to be very thick. Ice moves out of the Arctic through Baffin Bay, along the coast of eastern Greenland, and through the Bering Strait.

Ocean covered in sea ice in March 2018, when it began its annual melt, was at a record low, covering about one million square kilometers less than the long-term average. This is only part of the story, however. The well-documented late twentieth- and twenty-first-century warming trend also means that most of the sea ice in the Arctic Ocean is now new ice, only one to two years old. The extent of multi-year ice has declined, accounting for 34 percent of the total ice in the Arctic Ocean in 2018, down from 61 percent in 1984, according to the National Snow and Ice Data Center. Only 2 percent of that multi-year ice is judged to be more than five years in age. This development is significant because new ice tends to be 5–6.5 feet thick, while older ice can be 9.8–13.1 feet or more thick. The new, relatively thin ice is prone to breaking up in storms that are reaching the area in increasing frequency and to melting during the warmer months of the year.

Disappearing sea ice is also disrupting life for animals that depend on it, such as walrus, ringed seals, and polar bears, and it is challenging

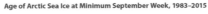

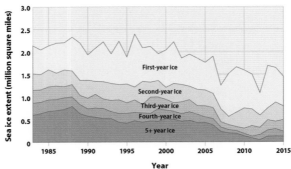

Figure 118   Age of Arctic Sea Ice at Minimum September Week, 1983–2015. This chart, made using data from the National Snow and Ice Data Center, shows the decline in sea ice generally, and in old ice in particular, since 1983. The oldest ice, five years and older, shows the steepest decline.

people who depend on stable ice to hunt marine mammals for food and to travel during the winter and spring. Hunters must use great caution when venturing out on the fast ice, for areas that were once safe to cross may no longer be stable.

In the warming Arctic, there are dramatic changes on land, too. Terrestrial vegetation is changing as trees and shrubs move north, taking advantage of a longer growing season and warmer soil. Coastlines throughout the region are being destabilized by the melting of permafrost, resulting in coastal erosion and slumping of the land. Coastal regions are further compromised by rising sea levels that leave them vulnerable to destructive storm surges and coastal erosion. Many of the coastal areas on which explorers and Inughuit used to camp in the 1900s are being destroyed, and today it would be nearly impossible to re-create Peary's 1908–1909 expedition because the icescape is so profoundly different.

Who Owns the Arctic?

Between 1886 and 1909, most of the known islands of the Canadian Arctic Archipelago (the islands north of the Canadian mainland) were claimed by Canada. West Greenland was a Danish colony, and northwestern Greenland remained unclaimed. Norwegian and American explorers were going to the Canadian Arctic Archipelago without asking any national or regional authority for permission to live, hunt, or explore the lands and their surrounding waters. During his 1899–1902 expedition, Otto Sverdrup discovered a series of islands in the Canadian Arctic Archipelago that he claimed for Norway, and in 1906 Norwegian explorer Roald Amundsen, on board the *Gjøa* on what he characterized as a scientific mission, completed the first transit of the Northwest Passage. Meanwhile, beginning in 1850, a long line of American explorers, including Elisha Kent Kane and Charles Francis Hall, preceded Peary into northwestern Greenland and explored islands in the Canadian Arctic Archipelago.

In the early 1900s, Canada grew quite concerned about the Norwegians' activities and Peary's ongoing work. Not only was Peary repeatedly establishing base camps on Canadian High Arctic islands and taking large quantities of game to feed people on his expeditions, but he was also naming geographic features after his financial backers. Canada and the United States had already experienced an unpleasant boundary dispute in Alaska. Would Canadian sovereignty be challenged in the eastern Arctic as well? As a result of these growing concerns, Joseph E. Bernier, captain of the CGS *Arctic*, spent considerable time in the Canadian Arctic Archipelago raising the Canadian flag wherever possible, physically and tangibly reinforcing Canada's claim to those islands. Finally, in 1930, Norway recognized Canada's sovereignty over the Sverdrup Islands.

On the Greenland side, in the early 1900s explorers and ethnographers Ludvig Mylius-Erichsen and Knud Rasmussen attempted to claim northwestern Greenland on behalf of Denmark, but Denmark showed little interest, and it was not until 1937 that Denmark claimed all of Greenland. During the Second World War, the United States took over administration of Greenland while Denmark was occupied, returning control to Denmark at the end of the war. In 1953, Greenland, which had been considered a colony, was declared an integral part of Denmark.

Today the Arctic is home to approximately four million people living in both rural and urban settings. The eight Arctic nations that ring the Arctic Ocean (the United States, Canada, Denmark [Greenland], Iceland, Norway, Sweden, Finland, and Russia) belong to an intergovernmental forum called the Arctic Council, created in part to manage those portions of the Arctic Ocean that fall outside any country's exclusive economic zone and resolve problems in the region in a peaceful manner. Sitting with them are seven organizations that represent all indigenous people of the Arctic. Non-Arctic nations with Arctic interests can become observers through an application process, and the number of nations seeking that status is growing every year.

Tiny, uninhabited Hans Island, which sits in the middle of Nares Strait, is the only disputed land in the region, claimed by both Canada and Denmark. Of more significance and consequence is the status of the Northwest Passage, considered an internal waterway by Canada (which shares oversight of the region with Inuit) but seen as an international waterway (and thus not subject to Canadian control) by a number of other countries, including the United States. Arctic nations are also busily mapping the continental shelf off their northern coasts in order to submit claims to sections of the Arctic Ocean as specified by the United Nations Convention on the Law of the Sea.

The warming of the Arctic and reduction in sea ice in the Arctic Ocean have generated considerable concern among scientists and northern residents and renewed worldwide interest in the Arctic by nations and organizations that see new opportunities developing. Increasing numbers of commercial and private vessels are navigating Arctic Ocean waters. Container vessels, bulk carriers, and energy exploration and extraction vessels, usually accompanied by icebreakers, move goods between Asia, Europe, and eastern North America; transport raw materials mined in the Arctic to southern processing centers; and seek new sources of gas and oil. Most vessels transiting the Arctic Ocean have been using the Northern Sea Route off the Russian coast, an area that is ice free more predictably than other parts of the Arctic Ocean, but recently the Northwest Passage also has been used. Tourists traveling in private yachts and aboard cruise ships are plying Arctic Ocean waters, including the Northwest Passage, in growing numbers. While commercial vessels bypass coastal communities, large cruise ships stop at designated locations, both creating economic opportunities and disrupting village life; the activities of private vessels are harder to monitor.

Management of shipping developments in an increasingly seasonally ice-free Arctic Ocean has become critically important. Protections for Arctic wildlife are of concern, as some species are becoming endangered by the warming Arctic, increased vessel traffic, persistent organic pollutants that have found their way north, and interest in a new Arctic fishery. The rights and welfare of local communities are too often forgotten in the rush to take advantage of a warming Arctic. Protection of hunting rights and activities, the development of sustainable businesses within northern communities, and food security issues are critically important, for the

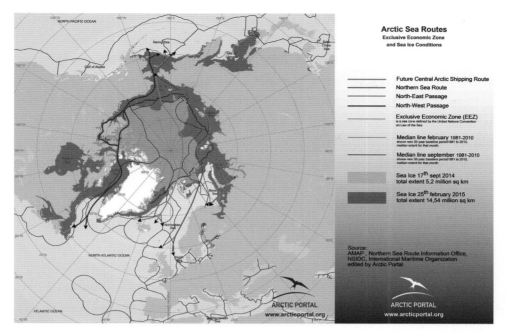

Figure 119 **Arctic Shipping.** Today, ships transit through the Arctic on the Northern Sea Route (red), the North-East Passage (pink) and the North-West Passage (green). In the not too distant future, some are already considering a route directly through the central Arctic Ocean, if not over the Pole itself (turquoise).

globalization, reflected in commercial shipping, provides few benefits to inhabitants of the Arctic.

As Arctic nations busily map the ocean floor extending from their continental shelves, the seabed below the North Pole remains an area of contention, with overlapping claims likely to come from Russia, Canada, and Denmark. Also, while the Arctic Council is committed to the peaceful resolution of disputes, tensions are developing, as is evident in the number of new or updated military bases and radar installations in the North and the various military exercises taking place there annually.

Indigenous Life

In the early 1900s, most Inuit groups inhabiting Greenland and Canada lived in extended family groups and led nomadic lives, harvesting food from the land and sea using their traditional technologies. Their versatile tool kits and sophisticated hunting strategies allowed them to hunt on land, in open water, and on ice. Inuit tended to frequent ecologically rich areas, successfully catching a broad range of terrestrial and marine animals for food, clothing, shelter, and transportation. Inuit throughout Canada and Greenland were used to having total autonomy, but no one consulted them when Western nations claimed Inuit homelands as their own.

Throughout the twentieth century, the descendants of Inuit who worked with Peary and other explorers were settled in permanent communities and experienced various traumas due to concerted efforts by missionaries, merchants, and government officials to assimilate them into Western lifestyles. Throughout the North, families (and sometimes entire communities) were forced to relocate to areas unfamiliar to them. For instance, the vibrant community of Hebron on the Labrador coast that had supplied Peary with wood in 1906, when the *Roosevelt* ran out of coal on its way south, was closed in 1959 in an effort to consolidate the Inuit community on the central Labrador coast. In northwestern Greenland, Inughuit from Ummannaq, some of whom had worked for Peary in their youth, were forced to abandon their homes and relocate to Qaanaaq in 1953 to make

Figure 120   Odaq Leaving His House in Qaanaaq. As an important elder in the community, Odaq, the most talented Inughuit to help Peary reach the North Pole, was one of the few who felt comfortable speaking out against the forced relocation of Inughuit families from Ummannaq to Qaanaaq in 1953. Despite his objections, the move went ahead. In Qaanaaq, people were given small, poorly insulated wooden houses that were difficult to keep warm, a poor substitute for the warm stone and sod houses they had left behind.

way for the United States' Thule Air Base, built on their land at the height of the Cold War. Also in 1953, in response to Canada's Cold War sovereignty concerns, families from Pond Inlet (on Baffin Island) and Inukjuak (in northern Quebec) were relocated to unoccupied Cornwallis Island and Ellesmere Island. The contemporary communities of Resolute Bay and Grise Fiord, now the northernmost communities in Canada, result from that forced relocation.

Today, Canadian Inuit have regained a certain amount of autonomy, largely as a result of land claims settlements that have improved their prospects for controlling their lives. In 1979, Greenland gained a Home Rule Government and then, in 2009, a Self Rule Government, giving the inhabitants of the region control over most matters of daily life, though Denmark retains control over international relations and the United States continues to operate the Thule Air Base, which has again become strategically important in world affairs.

Science and Communication

By the late 1800s, there was worldwide interest in better understanding how northern environmental phenomena functioned, as evidenced by the First International Polar Year (1882–1883) scientific expeditions at Fort Conger on Ellesmere Island and at Point Barrow (now Utqiagvik), Alaska. The gathering of environmental data was dependent on having accurate instruments operated by competent individuals. Collection of tidal and weather data required great diligence, as reflected in the tide measurements and temperature readings recorded multiple times a day by various assistants on Peary's expeditions. Scientists continue to study northern terrestrial and marine environments in the field, but they increasingly deploy arrays of sophisticated instruments that collect data they can access remotely. Inuit are finally being recognized for the depth and breadth of their traditional knowledge of northern environments, something that Peary understood well but few others have grasped.

During Peary's time, explorers communicated using word-of-mouth, letters, and notes. Explorers who embarked on multi-year expeditions might not be heard from for months or years unless they managed to get word out by way of a passing vessel. The first transatlantic cable was successfully laid across the Atlantic Ocean in 1858, revolutionizing the speed with which information could be communicated across the Atlantic, but the northernmost points in the North Atlantic with telegraph capacities during Peary's time were Indian Harbour and Battle Harbour in southern Labrador, as well as Lerwick in the Shetland Islands. Indeed, all three places played a role in the unfolding drama of competing North Pole claims made by Cook and Peary in 1909.

Technological advancements such as radio communication began to transform the Arctic in the 1920s, providing northern residents with new access to information and resources, as well as the ability to communicate with the south. Today northern communities are linked to the rest of the world via satellites, internet cables, and (in some places) cell towers. Vessels, researchers, and residents have come to rely on Global Positioning System technologies.

What would Peary have thought of such developments? He was deeply involved in exploring the possibilities of flight before he died, so in all likelihood he would have been delighted by the new technology. He might have been concerned about the status of American claims in the region, nodded approvingly at the Inughuit's continued astute use of their traditional and Western technologies, and been utterly delighted with the Global Positioning System—though no doubt he would have tried to improve its accuracy and performance.

AFTERWORD

Floeberg Beach

In 2011, the pilot at the controls of the Kenn Borek Air Ltd. plane that
flew us from the Polar Continental Shelf Program facility at Resolute Bay,
Nunavut, to Cape Sheridan was having difficulty finding a place to land.
As he circled the area, occasionally gently testing various river terraces
with the plane's wheels, we stared out the windows, transfixed by what
was below us. A landscape devoid of much vegetation lay adjacent to a
sea choked with jumbled ice that extended onto the shore. Then we spotted tent rings and rectangular outlines of what was left of crate houses,
along with various cairns and monuments left by the crews of the *Alert* in
1859 and the *Roosevelt* in 1905–1906 and 1908–1909.

When we first arrived at Cape Sheridan, the land was eerily quiet, save
for the occasional bird call, the buzzing of some furry bees, and the sound
of water lapping on the shore. Near the end of our visit, the sea ice began
to move, and suddenly the refrain "I can hear the ice running," which
appeared repeatedly in George Wardwell's journals, made sense. We could
hear the very distinct sound of ice on the move.

While we mapped and tested the remains of structures and walked
around the Floeberg Beach area, it was easy to imagine the *Roosevelt*
sitting offshore, a gangplank running from its deck to the landfast ice, and
teams of men, Inughuit and Westerners, coming and going by dog sledge,
while children played. We began to understand the stress experienced
by the Inughuit women living in tents in this foreign place, trying to care
for their families while eating strange food and burning smelly kerosene
lamps. When we visited the memorial erected in honor of Ross Marvin,
we could feel the sadness the men on the *Roosevelt* must have experienced as they built it. The sense of remoteness and wilderness was com-
pounded when we encountered a muskox clearly not happy to find our
camp in the way of its route down to the river.

While at Cape Sheridan we could see the northern coast of Greenland
to the east and the Canadian Forces Station Alert was discernable to the

Figure 121   Summer Sea Ice. Late summer ice floes crowd the shore at Floeberg Beach with the mountains of northern Greenland in the distance across Nares Strait. The strait is almost always choked with sea ice in constant motion due to tides and a southerly flowing current.

north. The occasional aircraft landing at Alert, all-terrain vehicle tire tracks, and the remains of weather balloons strewn over the area served to remind us that the Arctic known by Peary and his men was fundamentally different from the one in which we stood.

The flight to Cape Sheridan had dropped us into a landscape last occupied in the 1900s, while the flight back to Resolute Bay provided us with a bird's-eye view of contemporary challenges. In early August the sea was devoid of ice, which was alarming. We could see rivers discharging torrents of silt-laden water from massive glaciers melting in the summer heat, and we landed back in the hamlet of Resolute Bay, established during a forced relocation of Inuit and hosting a major Canadian military exercise during our stay.

The casual observer traveling through the landscapes we visited will see many things that outsiders have always said characterize the Arctic: expanses of land devoid of human-made structures, encounters with wild animals that may never have seen a human being, and awe-inspiring forces of nature witnessed against a big sky. By looking closely, we can see remains of past Inuit activities throughout the region and the profound social and environmental changes that are under way. That process of looking at contemporary developments parallels what we have tried to do in this book as we have studied manuscripts, photographs, and artifacts from the early 1900s. We have peered closely and lingered over certain works to better understand dimensions of Robert E. Peary's North Pole expeditions that have not been examined by the casual reader. And we have done our best to highlight the accomplishments of men and women largely neglected in the extensive North Pole–related literature.

This book uses modern spellings of Inughuit names. The following list gives the modern spelling with examples of how the names were spelled in the historic literature. The modern spellings are drawn from fieldwork conducted by Genevieve M. LeMoine, were provided by Navarana K'avigaq and David Qaavigaq, or were taken from Lyle Dick's book *Muskox Land* and from Kenn Harper's book *Give Me My Father's Body*.

Modern spelling	Historic spelling
Aapilaq	Ahpellah (Ahwela)
Aleqasina	Alakahsingwah, Ally
Aleqasinnguaq	Keshungwa
Anaukaq	Anowka
Ane	Ane, Annie
Aqattanguaq	Akatingwah
Atangana	Atangana
Amaunalik	Akmowneddy
Aviaq	A-wee-ah
Elatu	Elatu
Eqariusaq	Ekkaiasha
Equ	Arco (also Ikwa)
Iggianguaq	Egingwah
Inatdliaq	Inatdliaq
Inukittoq (also Inukitsuapaluk)	In-u-gee-tok (also Inyugeetoo or Harrigan)
Ittukusuk	Etookashoo
Kali, Kale	Kahda
Kudluktoq	Koodlooktoo
Kuutsikitoq	Kooeigeto
Minik	Mene
Mannik	Mane
Nuttak	Nooktaq

Modern spelling	Historic spelling
Odaq	Ootah
Ole	Ole, Odie
Panikpak	Panikpah
Piugattoq	Pewahtoo
Qaajuuttaq	Kai-otah, Kyutah
Qaaviguaq	Kiweea
Qaijunguaq	Clayingwah
Qarkutsiaq	Carko
Qisuk	Kishook
Qitdlarsuaq	Qitdlarsuaq
Samik	Sammie
Sigluk	Seeglo
Sipsu	Sipsoo
Uisaakkassak	Wesharkoopsi
Ukkaujaaq	Ooqueah

Photographs

A number of the men on the North Pole expeditions owned cameras and took photographs, understanding that Peary had the right to use them. Thus, many of the photographs credited to Peary were not taken by him. Some of the black-and-white images were turned into glass lantern slides that were expertly hand tinted. All the hand-tinted photographs in this book are held by the Peary-MacMillan Arctic Museum, most of them donated to the institution by Donald B. MacMillan, who used them when lecturing. Images can be found in a number of other institutions, including the National Archives and Records Administration, the National Geographic Society, and the Library of Congress.

Artifacts

There is no single repository of artifacts related to the North Pole; rather, a variety of museums care for North Pole–related objects. The scattering of artifacts is the result of two major factors: Peary's generosity, for he gave friends and major donors gifts of objects and equipment, and an auction of his daughter Marie's belongings upon her death. Among the institutions holding Peary-related artifacts are the Peary-MacMillan Arctic Museum, the Maine State Museum, the Berkshire Museum, the National Museum of American History, the American Museum of Natural History, and the Explorers Club. Significant objects are in private hands as well.

Robert Bartlett's family home, Hawthorne Cottage, located in Brigus, Newfoundland and Labrador, is a National Historic Site in Canada, overseen by Parks Canada. The Peary summer home on Eagle Island, in Harpswell, Maine, is a National Historic Landmark managed by Maine's Bureau of Parks and Lands.

Published First-Hand Accounts

There are six books (identified with an * in the bibliography) written by Peary and members of his 1905–1906 and 1908–1909 North Pole expeditions that are first-hand accounts of the men's experiences, as well as two books by Cook that are first-hand accounts of his 1907–1909 expedition. They are listed in the bibliography. These books are supplemented by vast archival resources.

Archival Sources

The majority of Peary's papers are at the National Archives and Records Administration in College Park, Maryland. Papers from Peary's early expeditions to Greenland are at the Academy of Natural Sciences at Drexel University in Philadelphia, Pennsylvania.

Papers of Peary's assistants are mostly held by institutions near their homes. Ross Marvin's papers are held by the Chemung Valley History Museum; John Goodsell's by the Mercer County Historical Society; Donald MacMillan's by the George J. Mitchell Department of Special Collections and Archives, Bowdoin College; George Borup's by the Archives of the American Geographical Society at the University of Wisconsin–Milwaukee; and Matthew Henson's by the Beulah M. Davis Special Collections at Morgan State University. Robert Bartlett's papers are held by the George J. Mitchell Department of Special Collections and Archives, Bowdoin College; the American Geographical Society; and the Bartlett family.

The papers of Josephine Peary and Marie Peary Stafford Khune are at the Maine Women Writers Collection at the University of New England. The papers of the Peary Arctic Club are held by the Explorers Club. George Wardwell's journals are held by his family and are on loan to the Peary-MacMillan Arctic Museum, Bowdoin College. Frederick Cook's papers are at the Library of Congress.

Secondary Sources

There are vast numbers of newspaper articles covering the North Pole controversy that can be found by accessing databases of archived newspapers. For an analysis of the media's role in the controversy, we relied on some of those archival materials as well as Beau Riffenburgh's 1994 book *The Myth of the Explorer*. Many books on Arctic exploration also reexamine the controversy.

Pertinent Articles and Books

Abramson, Howard S. 1991. *Hero in Disgrace: The Life of Arctic Explorer Frederick A. Cook*. Paragon House, New York.

Balch, Edwin Swift. 1913. *The North Pole and Bradley Land*. Campion and Company, Philadelphia.

Bartlett, Robert A. 1928. *The Log of Bob Bartlett: The True Story of Forty Years of Seafaring and Exploration*. G. P. Putnam's Sons, New York.

———. 1931. Bringing the Crippled *Roosevelt* Home. In *Told at the Explorers Club: True Tales of Modern Exploration*, edited by F. A. Blossom, pp. 29–52. Albert and Charles Boni, New York.

Bonanomi, Emma. 2013. To Be Black and American: Matthew Henson and His Post-Pole Lecture Tour, 1909–10. In *North by Degree: New Perspectives on Arctic Exploration*, edited by Susan A. Kaplan and Robert McCracken Peck, pp. 185–209. American Philosophical Society, Philadelphia.

*Borup, George. 1911. *A Tenderfoot with Peary*. 3rd ed. Frederick A. Stokes, New York.

Bryce, Robert M. 1997. *Cook & Peary: The Polar Controversy, Resolved*. Stackpole Books, Mechanicsburg, Pennsylvania.

———. 2015. "It Proves Falsehood Absolutely . . ." The Lost Notebook of Dr. Frederick A. Cook. *The Polar Record* 51(2):177–190.

*Cook, Frederick A. 1912 [1911]. *My Attainment of the Pole: Being the Record of the Expedition that First Reached the Boreal Center, 1907–1909. With a Final Summary of the Polar Controversy*. Mitchell Kennerley, New York, London.

*———. 1951. *Return from the Pole; edited, with an introduction, by Frederick J. Pohl*. Pellegrini & Cudahy, New York.

Counter, S. Allen. 2018 [1991]. *North Pole Legacy: The Search for the Arctic Offspring of Robert Peary and Matthew Henson*. Skyhorse Publishing, New York (reprint edition).

Dick, Lyle. 2001. *Muskox Land: Ellesmere Island in the Age of Contact*. University of Calgary Press, Calgary.

———. 2004. Robert Peary's North Polar Narratives and the Making of an American Icon. *American Studies* 45(2):5–34.

Eames, Hugh. 1973. *Winner Lose All: Dr. Cook and the Theft of the North Pole*. Little, Brown, and Company, Boston.

Erikson, Patricia Pierce. 2009. Josephine Diebitsch Peary (1863–1955). *Arctic* 62(1):102–104.

———. 2013. Homemaking, Snowbabies, and the Search for the North Pole: Josephine Diebitsch Peary and the Making of National History. In *North by Degree: New Perspectives on Arctic Exploration*, edited by Susan A. Kaplan and Robert McCracken Peck, pp. 257–288. American Philosophical Society, Philadelphia.

Fitzgerald, Bertram A., Jr., ed. 1969. The Life of Matthew Henson. *Golden Legacy: Illustrated History Magazine*, vol. 5. Fitzgerald Publishing Co., St. Albans, New York.

*Goodsell, John W. 1983. *On Polar Trails: The Peary Expedition to the North Pole, 1908–09*. Eakin Press, Austin, Texas.

Hall, Thomas F. 1917. *Has the North Pole Been Discovered? An Analytical and Synthetical Review of the Published Narratives of the Two Arctic Explorers, Dr. Frederick A. Cook and Civil Engineer Robert E. Peary U.S.N.: Also a Review of the Action of the U.S. Government*. Richard G. Badger, Boston.

Harper, Kenn. 2000 [1986]. *Give Me My Father's Body: The Life of Minik, the New York Eskimo*. Steerforth Press, South Royalton, Vermont.

———. 2007. Robert Peary and the Inuit. *Nunatsiaq News* (April 26).

Hayes, J. Gordon. 1929. *Robert Edwin Peary: A Record of His Explorations 1886–1909*. Grant Richards & Humphrey Toulmin, London.

———. 1934. *The Conquest of the North Pole: Recent Arctic Exploration*. Thornton Butterworth, London.

Henderson, Bruce. 2005. *True North: Peary, Cook, and the Race to the Pole*. W. W. Norton, New York.

*Henson, Matthew A. 1912. *A Negro Explorer at the North Pole*. Library of American Civilization. Frederick A. Stokes, New York.

Hobbs, William Herbert. 1936. *Peary*. Macmillan, New York.

Huntington, P. A. M. 2002. Robert E. Peary and the Cape York Meteorites. *Polar Geography* 26(1):53–65.

Kane, Elisha Kent. 1857. *Arctic Explorations: The Second Grinnell Expedition in Search of Sir John Franklin, 1853, '54, '55*. 2 vols. Childs & Peterson, Philadelphia.

Kaplan, Susan A., and Robert McCracken Peck, eds. 2013. *North by Degree: New Perspectives on Arctic Exploration*. American Philosophical Society, Philadelphia.

LeMoine, Genevieve M., Susan A. Kaplan, and Christyann M. Darwent. 2016. Living on the Edge: Inughuit Women and Geography of Contact. *Arctic* 69(5):1–12.

Lewin, W. Henry. 1911. *Did Peary Reach the Pole? By an Englishman in the Street.* Simpkin, Marshall, Hamilton, Kent & Co., London.

*MacMillan, Donald Baxter. 2008 [1934]. *How Peary Reached the Pole.* Reprint with new introduction by Genevieve M. LeMoine, Susan A. Kaplan, and Anne Witty. McGill-Queen's University Press, Montreal and Kingston.

Mirsky, Jeannette. 1948 [1934]. *To the Arctic! The Story of Northern Exploration from Earliest Times to the Present.* A. A. Knopf, New York.

Nares, George S. 1878. *Narrative of a Voyage to the Polar Sea during 1875–6 in H.M. Ships "Alert" and "Discovery."* S. Low, Marston, Searle, & Rivington, London.

Peary, Josephine Diebitsch. 1894. *My Arctic Journal: A Year among Ice-Fields and Eskimos.* Contemporary Publishing Co., New York.

Peary, Robert E. 1898. *Northward Over the "Great Ice": A Narrative of Life and Work along the Shores and upon the Interior Ice-Cap of Northern Greenland in the Years 1886 and 1891–1897.* Frederick A. Stokes, New York.

———. 1903a. Four Years' Arctic Exploration, 1898–1902. *Geographic Journal* 22(6):646–668.

———. 1903b. Sledging over the Polar Pack. *Outing* 41(4):395–406.

*———. 1907. *Nearest the Pole: A Narrative of the Polar Expedition of the Peary Arctic Club in the SS* Roosevelt, *1905–06.* Doubleday, Page & Company, New York.

———. 1910a. The Discovery of the North Pole, *Hampton's Magazine*, vol. 24 (January to September).

*———. 1910b. *The North Pole: Its Discovery in 1909 under the Auspices of the Peary Arctic Club.* Frederick A. Stokes, New York.

———. 1917. *The Secrets of Polar Travel.* The Century Co., New York.

Rawlins, Dennis. 1973. *Peary at the North Pole: Fact or Fiction?* R. B. Luce, Washington.

Riffenburgh, Beau. 1994. *The Myth of the Explorer: The Press, Sensationalism, and Geographic Discovery.* Oxford University Press, Oxford.

Robinson, Bradley. 1947. *Dark Companion.* K. M. McBride, New York.

Robinson, Michael F. 2006. *The Coldest Crucible: Arctic Exploration and American Culture.* University of Chicago Press, Chicago.

―――. 2015. Manliness and Exploration: The Discovery of the North Pole. *Osiris* 30(1):89–109.

Stam, Deirdre C. 2009. Introduction to *Matthew A. Henson's Historic Arctic Journey: The Classic Account of One of the World's Greatest Black Explorers*, pp. 3–53. Lyons Press, Guilford, Connecticut.

―――. 2017. Interpreting Captain Bob Bartlett's AGS Notebook Chronicling Significant Parts of Peary's 1908–09 North Pole Expedition. *Geographic Review* 107(1):185–206.

Weems, John Edward. 1960. *Race for the Pole*. Henry Holt, New York.

―――. 1967. *Peary, the Explorer and the Man: Based on His Personal Papers*. Houghton Mifflin, Boston.

All photographs and objects are from the collection of the Peary-
MacMillan Arctic Museum unless otherwise noted. All others are used
with permission.

Figure 1: Unidentified photographer, *Robert Peary on Return from the North
Pole*, Ellesmere Island 1909. Gift of Donald and Miriam MacMillan. 3000.32.1801.

Figure 2: Josephine Diebitsch Peary, *Peary's North Pole Flag*, ca. 1898. Courtesy
of the National Geographic Society. Photograph by Mark Hensley.

Figure 3: Unidentified photographer, *Portrait of Charles Nutter Peary and Mary
W. Peary*, ca. 1855. Museum purchase. 1996.12.2. Photograph by Mark Hensley.

Figure 4: Unidentified photographer, *Portrait of Robert E. Peary, age 3*, 1859.
Museum purchase. 1996.12.5. Photograph by Mark Hensley.

Figure 5: Unidentified maker, *Robert Peary's Delta Kappa Epsilon Pin*, ca. 1875.
Loan from DKE Fraternity. AML4.1973. Photograph by Mark Hensley.

Figure 6: Robert E. Peary, *Snowy Owl Mount*, Brunswick, ca. 1875. Bowdoin
College Collection, presented by Dr. J. W. Curtis. Photograph by Mark Hensley.

Figure 7: Wm. Pierce, A. O. Reed, Photographers, *Robert E. Peary, Bowdoin
Graduation Photo*, Brunswick, 1877. Albumen print. 1998.1.16.

Figure 8: Unidentified maker, *Steel Engineer's Chain Used by Robert E. Peary*,
ca. 1878. Gift of the Pejepscot Historical Society. 1990.16.6. Photograph by Mark
Hensley.

Figure 9: Robert E. Peary, *Map of Fryeburg, Maine, in 1897*. Courtesy of the
Fryeburg Historical Society.

Figure 10: Unidentified photographer, *Robert E. Peary in Nicaragua*, ca. 1885.
NARA RG401 XP-XPD-15-3.

Figure 11: G. V. Buck, *Josephine Diebitsch Peary*, Washington, D.C., ca. 1890.
Platinum print. 1998.1.17.

Figure 12: Donald Baxter MacMillan, *Matthew Henson on Deck by Sledges,
Aboard the* Roosevelt, 1908–1909. Gift of Donald and Miriam MacMillan.
3000.1.63.

Figure 13: Unidentified photographer, *"The Days were very long" [Peary with broken leg], Northward Over the Great Ice*, p. 79.

Figure 14: Robert E. Peary, *Navy Cliff, North Greenland*, July, 1892. NARA RG401_XRP-1981B-257.

Figure 15: Unidentified photographer, *The Meteorite* Ahnighito *Being Unloaded from the* Hope. New York, 1897. The Stewart Collection of Capt. John Bartlett's Photographs. 1988.2.37.

Figure 16: Unidentified photographer, *The Six New York Eskimos with Albert Operti on the Deck of the* Hope. *(l-r) Nuttak, Atangana, Minik, Qisuk, Aviaq, and Uisaakkassak.* 1897. The Stewart Collection of Capt. John Bartlett's Photographs. 1988.2.41.

Figure 17: John J. Costinett, *U.S. Navy Admiral's Dress Jacket and Trousers, R.E. Peary*, Washington, D.C., ca. 1911. Gift of the Pejepscot Historical Society. 1990.16.11; Joseph Starkey, *Epaulettes of RAMD Horne*, London, ca. 1910. Courtesy of the Naval Historical Center; Warnoch Co., *U.S. Navy Sword, Engraved R.E. Peary*, New York, ca. 1911. Courtesy of Robert Peary, III. AML1993.3.8. Photograph by Mark Hensley.

Figure 18: Lester M. Hart, *Peary's Summer Home*, Eagle Island, 1909–1910. Arctic Museum Collection. 3000.39.1.

Figure 19: Unidentified photographer, *Robert E. Peary Demonstrating a Flying Costume*, 1914–1915. NARA RG401XP-XPF-9.

Figure 20: Donald Baxter MacMillan, *S.S.* Roosevelt *and the* Erik *[in fore-ground]*, Etah, 1908. Gift of Donald and Miriam MacMillan. 3000.32.1762.

Figure 21: Donald Baxter MacMillan, *S.S.* Roosevelt *in the Ice*, 1908–1909. Gift of Donald and Miriam MacMillan. 3000.32.1126.

Figure 22: Frédéric Dussault, *Floeberg Beach*, Ellesmere Island, July 30, 2011. Courtesy of the Cape Sheridan Archaeological Project. cs2011_7_30_53.

Figure 23: Unidentified photographer, *"Sewing Bee" [Women Sewing on the Deck of the* Roosevelt*]*, 1908–1909. NARA RG401XP-XPS 7-1.

Figure 24: Donald Baxter MacMillan, *Teams on Rough Ice in the Polar Sea*, Arctic Ocean, 1909. Gift of Donald and Miriam MacMillan. 3000.33.205.

Figure 25: Mellie Dunham, *Snowshoes Used by Donald MacMillan*, Norway, Maine, ca. 1908. Gift of Donald and Miriam MacMillan. 1000.83.a&b.

Figure 26: Robert E. Peary, *Sketch for Snowshoe Slipper*, ca. 1890. NARA RG401 XP-XPAR-Folder 1.

Figure 27: Fitzhugh Green, *MacMillan at Peary Cairn*, Axel Heiberg Island, May 1914. Gift of Donald and Miriam MacMillan. 3000.32.1223.

Figure 28: Unidentified photographer, *Lowering a New Rudder*, Cape Union, Ellesmere Island, July 28, 1906. NARA RG401XPR 245A.

Figure 29: Unidentified photographer, *Shattered Stern of SS* Roosevelt, Etah, 1906. Gift of Donald and Miriam MacMillan. 3000.32.1962.

Figure 30: Unidentified photographer, *The Deck of the* Roosevelt *with Wood for Fuel*, Labrador Sea, fall 1906. NARA RG401 XPR 245B.

Figure 31: Donald Baxter MacMillan, *Hunting Party, Camped*, fall 1908. Gift of Donald and Miriam MacMillan. 3000.32.1785.

Figure 32: Fauth & Co., *Theodolite*. Washington, D.C., ca. 1900. Gift of Marie Peary Kuhne. 1967.184. Photograph by Mark Hensley.

Figure 33: Donald Baxter MacMillan, *Good Going! [Dogs Pulling Sledge]*. Gift of Donald and Miriam MacMillan. 3000.32.12.

Figure 34: Unidentified photographer, *Games on the Polar Sea*, Arctic Ocean, 1909. Gift of Donald and Miriam MacMillan. 3000.33.200.

Figure 35: Matthew A. Henson, *Four Eskimos at the Pole [Seegloo, Ootah (Odaq), Egingwah, and Ooqueeah]*, April 1909. Gift of Donald and Miriam MacMillan. 3000.32.1822.

Figure 36: Robert E. Peary, *American Flag and Sledges at the Pole*, April 1909. Gift of Donald and Miriam MacMillan. 3000.32.1824.

Figure 37: Keuffel & Esser Co., *Pocket Compass*, New York, ca. 1908. Gift of Marie Peary Kuhne. 1967.253. Photograph by Mark Hensley.

Figure 38: Waltham Watch Co., *Twenty-Four Hour Watch Used by MacMillan*, Waltham, ca. 1908. Gift of Miriam Look MacMillan. 1976.1. Photograph by Mark Hensley.

Figure 39: Josephine Peary and unidentified maker, *Peary's Wool Undershirt*. Gift of the Pejepscot Historical Society. 1990.16.16. Photograph by Mark Hensley.

Figure 40: Unidentified photographer, *Ross Gilmore Marvin in Furs*, 1905–1909. Gift of Miriam Look MacMillan. 1994.5.2862.

Figure 41: Donald Baxter MacMillan, *Cross Erected for Loss of Ross Marvin*. Gift of Donald and Miriam MacMillan. 3000.32.1111.

Figure 42: Susan A. Kaplan, *Ross Marvin Memorial Plaque*, Cape Sheridan, Ellesmere Island, July 28, 2011. Courtesy of the Cape Sheridan Archaeological Project. cs201_7_28_34.

Figure 43: Robert E. Peary, *Toboggan Design*, February 9, 1886. NARA RG401 XPU 3-5.

Figure 44: Unidentified photographer, *Coasting [Peary posing on sledge]*, Washington, D.C., 1886. NARA RG401 XPS 2-2.

Figure 45: Emil Diebitsch, *Peary's Lodge, Rear [Red Cliff House]*, MacCormick Fjord, 1892. Gift of Edward Peary Stafford. 2000.10.24.

Figure 46: Robert E. Peary, *Notes on [Ah-go-tok-suah?] Sledge No 4*. NARA RG401 A-1 Box 9 folder 15.

Figure 47: Unidentified photographer, *Sledge on Deck*, 1891–1892. NARA RG401 XP-XPU 3-1 (1891-2 Albumen Prints).

Figure 48: Robert E. Peary, *Mahatia Sledge*, January 19, 1895. NARA RG401 A-1 Box 9 folder 18.

Figure 49: Unidentified photographer, *Two Men on the Ice, MacMillan at Left*. Arctic Ocean, 1909. Gift of Donald and Miriam MacMillan. 3000.32.1116.

Figure 50: Robert E. Peary, *Notes on Sledge Loads*, ca. 1900. NARA RG401 A-1 Box 14 Envelope: Field Notes Peary 1899–1901.

Figure 51: Robert E. Peary, *Sketch for Cooker*, 1898. NARA RG401 A-1 Box 17 Folder: Misc. Expedition planning 1898.

Figure 52: Robert E. Peary, *Ice Melter Sketch*, 1906. NARA RG401 A-1 Box 19 Folder: Misc. maps and drawings.

Figure 53: Robert E. Peary, Roosevelt *Drawing, Angle of Bow*, ca. 1904. NARA RG401-1 Box 24 Folder 7: Roosevelt Drawings and Specs.

Figure 54: Robert E. Peary, Roosevelt *Bracing Scheme*, January 27, 1904. NARA RG401-1 Box 24 Folder 7: Roosevelt Drawings and Specs.

Figure 55: Unidentified photographer, *The* Roosevelt *Stern, in Dry Dock*, 1905–1908. In Memory of Reginald Wilcox and Captain David C. Nutt. 2010.2.292.

Figure 56: Frédéric Dussault, *Susan A. Kaplan and Genevieve M. LeMoine Examining the Remains of Peary's Crate Houses*, Floeberg Beach, Ellesmere Island, July 30, 2011. Courtesy of the Cape Sheridan Archaeological Project, cs2011_7_30_51.

Figure 57: Donald Baxter MacMillan, *My Men, Cape Morris Jesup Trip [The Cape Jesup Grenadiers]*, Cape Morris Jesup, Greenland, spring 1909. Gift of Donald and Miriam MacMillan. 3000.33.2004.

Figure 58: Donald Baxter MacMillan, *Sledges, A Long Line. North Pole Expedition*, Ellesmere Island, 1908–1909. Gift of Donald and Miriam MacMillan. 3000.32.1061.

Figure 59: Matthew Henson and Robert E. Peary, *The Hubbard Sledge*, 1908. Arctic Museum Collection. 1966.157. Photograph by Dennis Griggs.

Figure 60: Unidentified photographer, *Borup, MacMillan at Battle Harbor, Labrador,* Battle Harbour, 1909. Gift of Donald and Miriam MacMillan. 3000.32.1112.

Figure 61: Robert E. Peary, *Camp Site, Josephine Peary Standing,* 1891–1892. Museum purchase. 2005.12.22.

Figure 62: Rice, *The Snow Baby,* ca. 1894. Gift of Louise Minot. 2007.11.

Figure 63: Henry G. Bryant, *Miss Bill Before,* Aboard the *Falcon,* 1894. From the American Geographical Society Library, University of Wisconsin-Milwaukee Libraries.

Figure 64: Henry G. Bryant, *Miss Bill After,* Aboard the *Falcon,* 1894. From the American Geographical Society Library, University of Wisconsin–Milwaukee Libraries.

Figure 65: Emil Diebitsch, *Bill and Marie Peary in Doorway,* Philadelphia, 1894–1895. Gift of Edward Peary Stafford. 2000.10.245.

Figure 66: John Bartlett, *Bill and Four Polar Eskimos (l-r) Eqariusaq, Nuttak, Aviaq? and two unidentified women,* Bowdoin Bay, Greenland, 1895. The Stewart Collection of Capt. John Bartlett's Photographs. 1988.2.47.

Figure 67: Donald Baxter MacMillan, *"Bill" Chewing a Boot-Sole [aboard S.S. Roosevelt],* 1908–1909. Gift of Donald and Miriam MacMillan. 3000.32.59.

Figure 68: Unidentified photographer, *Josephine Peary at Home with Arctic Tableau,* Philadelphia or New York, 1890–1910. Gift of Wendy L. Noyes. 2015.6.

Figure 69: Emil Diebitsch, *Matthew Henson (l) with Group of Inuit on Rocks,* northwestern Greenland, 1892–1894. Gift of Edward Peary Stafford. 2000.10.327.

Figure 70: Donald Baxter MacMillan, *Henson in Furs, on Deck,* Aboard the *Roosevelt,* 1908–1909. Gift of Donald and Miriam MacMillan. 3000.32.1783.1.

Figure 71: *Chicago Sun-Times, Matthew Henson Receives Gold Medal from Chicago Geographic Society,* Chicago, 1948. Gift of Miriam Look MacMillan. 1994.5.2565.

Figure 72: Albert Operti, *Matthew Henson, Hassan Tobacco Card,* ca. 1910. Museum Purchase. 2000.19.

Figure 73: U.S. Postal Service, *First Day Cover, Gold Stamp Replica of Peary & Henson North Pole,* North Pole, Alaska, May 28, 1986. In memory of Dr. H. Franklin Williams. 2000.1.110.

Figure 74: Donald Baxter MacMillan, *Robert Bartlett*, Littleton Island, Greenland, 1908–1909. Gift of Donald and Miriam MacMillan. 3000.32.1805.

Figure 75: Reginald Wilcox, *Marie Peary Stafford, Robert A. Bartlett, Odaq (in white anorak), Qisuk, Inuit youngster at the Peary Monument*, Cape York, 1932. Gift of David Nutt Jr. 1994.10.6.

Figure 76: Kudluktoq, *George Borup, Kai-o-tah, and Donald MacMillan*, Cape Washington, Greenland, spring 1909. Gift of Donald and Miriam MacMillan. 3000.32.1102.

Figure 77: George Borup, *Two Eskimo Men [Sigloo and Ooqueah] at Cape Columbia Cairn with Sign Post*, Ellesmere Island, 1908–1909. Gift of Donald and Miriam MacMillan. 3000.32.1759.

Figure 78: Unidentified photographer, *Dr. John Goodsell*, Battle Harbour, September 1909. Arctic Museum Collection.

Figure 79: Samson Simeone, *Frédéric Dussault Excavating*, Floeberg Beach, Ellesmere Island, August 4, 2011. Courtesy of the Cape Sheridan Archaeological Project. cs2011_8_4_52.

Figure 80: Donald Baxter MacMillan, *Eskimos in Front of Igloo*, Nerky [Neqe], Greenland, 1924. Gift of Miriam and Donald MacMillan. 3000.33.1114.

Figure 81: Donald Baxter MacMillan, *Group in Front of Tupik [Inn-you-gee-to's family by Tupik]*, Nerky [Neqe], Greenland, 1925. Gift of Donald and Miriam MacMillan. 3000.32.978.

Figure 82: Donald Baxter MacMillan, *Building an Igloo*, Arctic Ocean, 1914. Gift of Donald and Miriam MacMillan. 3000.32.4.

Figure 83: Donald Baxter MacMillan, *Pulling Out a Narwhal*, northwestern Greenland, 1913–1917. Gift of Donald and Miriam MacMillan. 3000.32.1017.

Figure 84: Donald Baxter MacMillan, *Dovekies, Netting*, Etah, Greenland, 1913–1917. Gift of Donald and Miriam MacMillan. 3000.32.2038.

Figure 85: Donald Baxter MacMillan, *Walrus Hunting at Edge of Ice*. Gift of Donald and Miriam MacMillan. 3000.32.863.

Figure 86: Unidentified Inuit Artist, *Lamp [Quilliq]*. Gift of Donald and Miriam MacMillan. 1966.64. Photograph by Mark Hensley.

Figure 87: Donald Baxter MacMillan, *Teakettle over Flame*, northwestern Greenland, 1938. Gift of Miriam Look MacMillan. 1994.5.1003.

Figure 88: Donald Baxter MacMillan, *Eskimo Woman Scraping Skins with an Ulu*, northwestern Greenland, 1923–1925. Gift of Donald and Miriam MacMillan. 3000.33.1131.

Figure 89: Donald Baxter MacMillan, *"Our Eskimos" [Back l-r Qaavigaq, Ittukusuk, Amaunalik, Qaarqutsiannguaq, Kuutsikitoq. Front l-r Qianjunnguaq, Ane Petersen holding Ole, Atangana with Inatdliaq, Aviaq Henson]*, July 20, 1924. Gift of Donald and Miriam MacMillan. 3000.33.1110.

Figure 90: Dick Sears, *MacMillan, George Borup, Tom Gushue & Matt Henson [seated] by Sledge on the* Roosevelt, Battle Harbour, September 16, 1909. Gift of Donald and Miriam MacMillan. 3000.9.7.

Figure 91: Unidentified Inughuit Seamstress, *Caribou Parka [MacMillan's North Pole Outfit]*, 1908–1909. Gift of Donald and Miriam MacMillan. 1966.129.1. Photograph by Mark Hensley.

Figure 92: Unidentified Inughuit Seamstress, *Polar Bear Pants [MacMillan's North Pole Outfit]*, 1908–1909. Gift of Donald and Miriam MacMillan. 1966.129.2. Photograph by Mark Hensley.

Figure 93: George Borup, *Kyutah, Goodsell, Keshungwah and Inighito*, 1908–1909. Gift of Donald and Miriam MacMillan. 3000.1.99.

Figure 94: Emil Diebitsch, *Three Inuit Women*, northwestern Greenland, 1892–1894. Gift of Edward Peary Stafford. 2000.10.52.

Figure 95: Donald Baxter MacMillan, *Samik*, northwestern Greenland, ca. 1909. Gift of Donald and Miriam MacMillan. 3000.32.1773.

Figure 96: Donald Baxter MacMillan, *Sammy on Board the* Bowdoin, Bushman Island, August 10, 1924. Gift of Donald and Miriam MacMillan. 3000.33.1441.

Figure 97: Donald Baxter MacMillan, *Kadah [Kale Peary]*, Etah, 1913–1917. Gift of Donald and Miriam MacMillan. 3000.33.1068.

Figure 98: Rutherford Platt, *Kale Peary*, Herbert Island, August 1954. Gift of Alexander D. Platt '66. 2014.10.221.

Figure 99: Donald Baxter MacMillan, *Ah-now-ka*, Refuge Harbor, August 11, 1924. Gift of Donald and Miriam MacMillan. 3000.33.1030.

Figure 100: Donald Baxter MacMillan, *Anaqaq Henson*, Aboard the *Bowdoin*, 1938. Gift of Miriam Look MacMillan. 1994.5.1027.

Figure 101: William Hohenstein, *Dr. Frederick Cook*, Brooklyn, 1911. Library of Congress, https://www.loc.gov/item/98502700/.

Figure 102: Frederick Cook, *Ittukusuk and Aapilaq with Sledge*, 1908. Byrd Polar Research Center Library, http://go.osu.edu/frederickcook.

Figure 103: Robert E. Peary, *Telegram Sent to Associated Press*, New York, September 6, 1909. Gift of Melvin E. Stone III. 1996.24.1.

Figure 104: Boston American, *Peary on the* Roosevelt, Battle Harbour, September 1909. Gift of Donald and Miriam MacMillan. 3000.1.4.

Figure 105: North Pole Pub. Co., *Lapel Tag, "I Am for Peary / I Am for Cook,"* Auburn, Maine, 1909. Museum Purchase. 2006.5.3. Photograph by Mark Hensley.

Figure 106: Unknown maker, *Souvenir Mug of Robert E. Peary.* Gift of Donald and Miriam MacMillan. 1966.149. Photograph by Mark Hensley.

Figure 107: United States Tobacco Co., *North Pole Tobacco Tin.* Museum purchase. 1992.26.1. Photograph by Mark Hensley.

Figure 108: *Le Petit Journal, La Conquete du Pole Nord: Le docteur Cook et le commandant Peary s'en disputent la glorie,* Paris, September 19, 1909. Gift of Mr. William J. Nightingale, Class of 1951. 2001.17.

Figure 109: Frederick Cook, *North Pole Camp,* Arctic Ocean, April 1908. Library of Congress, https://www.loc.gov/item/2001695567/.

Figure 110: Robert E. Peary, *North Pole Flag and Sledges at the Pole,* Arctic Ocean, April 6–7, 1909. Gift of Donald and Miriam MacMillan. 3000.32.1823.

Figure 111: Canadian Camp, *Menu for Banquet Honoring Peary,* New York, March 5, 1910. Museum Purchase. 1990.11.2.

Figure 112: Unidentified photographer, *Donald MacMillan and Marie Stafford Aboard the S.S.* Peary, possibly Wiscasset, Maine, 1925. Gift of Miriam Look MacMillan, 1994.5.2452.

Figure 113: U.S. Navy, *USS* Skate *(SSN 578) Surfaces,* North Pole, 1959. http://navylive.dodlive.mil/2015/03/16/navyinnovates-arctic-operations-with-uss -skate-ssn-578/. (The appearance of U.S. Department of Defense [DoD] visual information does not imply or constitute DoD endorsement.)

Figure 114: U.S. Postal Service, *First Day Cover, Arctic Explorations Stamp,* Cresson, Pennsylvania, April 6, 1959. Arctic Museum Collection. 1000.32.4.

Figure 115: NOAA, *North Pole Webcam Image,* June 8, 2010, 8:25 pm. Courtesy of NOAA/Pacific Marine Environmental Laboratory, https://www.pmel.noaa.gov/ arctic-zone/gallery_np_moods.php.

Figure 116: Donald Baxter MacMillan, *Men on Pressure Ridge, North Pole Trip,* Arctic Ocean, spring 1909. Gift of Donald and Miriam MacMillan. 3000.32.1825.

Figure 117: AMAP, Icelandic Marine Institute, *Map of Arctic Currents,* 2010. Courtesy of Arctic Portal, http://library.arcticportal.org/id/eprint/1494.

Figure 118: U.S. EPA, *Age of Arctic Ice at Minimum September Week,* 1983–2015. https://www.epa.gov/climate-indicators/climate-change-indicators-arctic-sea-ice.

Figure 119: Arctic Portal, *Northern Sea Route and Sea Ice Conditions 2014–2015*. Courtesy of Arctic Portal, https://arcticportal.org/maps-shipping.

Figure 120: Donald Baxter MacMillan, *Odaq Outside His House*, Qaanaaq, 1954. Gift of Donald and Miriam MacMillan. 3000.34.1856.

Figure 121: Genevieve M. LeMoine, *Ice at Floeberg Beach*, Ellesmere Island, August 3, 2011. Courtesy of the Cape Sheridan Archaeological Project. cs2011_8_3_25.

ACKNOWLEDGMENTS

We have been conducting research on various facets of Robert E. Peary's career for more than 25 years. Our work has taken us on a number of journeys, physically and figuratively. We visited many of the far-flung places Peary frequented (although not the North Pole itself) as well as archives and museums housing relevant collections. As we endeavored to understand the mindsets of the Westerners and Inughuit involved on the North Pole expeditions and the challenges they faced, we scrutinized expedition journals, correspondence, and photographs that took us back in time, and we talked with descendants of expedition members on both sides of the North Atlantic. We could not have accomplished this work without the generous assistance and kindnesses of countless institutions and individuals.

Since 1987, Kane Lodge Foundation, Inc., under the direction of Peter Sulick and the late John Stichter, has supported 11 of our Peary-related projects. The Foundation funded conservation of some of the scientific instruments used on Peary's expeditions, preservation of Peary-related photograph collections, research trips to archives, two symposia, a traveling exhibition of Peary photographs, the *Arctic Explorers in Motion* film festival, the republication of Donald MacMillan's *How Peary Reached the Pole*, the publication of the *North by Degree* symposium papers, and a major inventory of the Peary Eagle Island house, conducted by two Bowdoin College students on behalf of the State of Maine.

In 2007, the Institute of Museum and Library Services awarded the Arctic Museum a Museums for America grant (MA-02-07-0230-07) that supported research, exhibition, conservation, and outreach activities related to the Arctic Museum's exhibit, *Northward Over the Great Ice: Robert E. Peary and the Quest for the North Pole*. The Edgard and Geraldine Feder Foundation, Inc., and Yves Feder in particular, helped Arctic Museum staff develop the audio components of the exhibition. Donors to Bowdoin's Friends of the College Fund supported the museum's outreach initiatives.

In 2011, with funding from the National Science Foundation's Office of Polar Programs, Arctic Social Science program (ARC-1134811), we flew to Cape Sheridan, on the northeast corner of Ellesmere Island, Nunavut, where, in both 1905–1906 and 1908–1909, Peary anchored the *Roosevelt* and established base camps. The opportunity to gain first-hand knowledge of the landscape and archaeologically investigate the region contributed greatly to our understanding of Peary's North Pole expeditions and the stresses people experienced. We would like to thank Anna Kerttula de Echave of the National Science Foundation and Margaret Berttuli of Parks Canada for encouraging us, and the amazing Ken Borek pilots and staff of the Polar Continental Shelf Program in Resolute Bay for their logistical support. Frédéric Dussault helped with excavations and made sure we ate well, and Samson Simeone, our polar bear guard, kept us safe.

Through Gibbons Summer Research Program fellowships, two students worked on aspects of the *Northward Over the Great Ice* exhibition. Zoe Eddy (Class of 2010) created an online interactive summary of Peary's expeditions, and Hillary Hooke (Class of 2009) began a daily historic blog of what happened exactly 100 years before, based on excerpts from the journals of various North Pole expedition members.

Our ability to conduct and sustain the many years of research that has resulted in exhibitions, academic articles and papers, public talks, and this publication was made possible thanks to the Russell and Janet Doubleday Endowment that underwrites most of the Peary-MacMillan Arctic Museum and Arctic Studies Center's budget.

Access to archives, museums, and historic sites was critical to our work, as was the assistance of their staffs. In Maine, we would like to thank Cally Gurley of the Maine Women Writers Collection of the University of New England; Gabriele Daniello of the Maine Historical Society; Sheila MacDonald of the Maine State Museum; and the staffs of the Fryeburg Historical Society, Cliff Island Historical Society, Castine Historical Society, Pejepscot Historical Society, Bucksport Historical Society, Buck Memorial Library, and Peary's Eagle Island. Our colleagues at the Bowdoin College Library and the George J. Mitchell Department of Special Collections and Archives have been of great assistance to us throughout the years, particularly Richard Lindemann and Caroline Moseley, who helped us in the early stages of our work.

Farther afield, James Zeender of the National Archives and Records Administration, Nancy Beers Parsons of the National Geographic Society,

Peter Lewis of the American Geographical Society, Amy Wilson and Rachel Dworkin of the Chemung County Historical Society, Christy Hunter Hall and Bill Philson of the Mercer County Historical Society, Clare Flemming and Dorothea Sartain of the Explorers Club, Barbara Mathé of the American Museum of Natural History, and Karen France of the Naval Historic Center facilitated our work with collections housed in their facilities. The staffs of the Battle Harbour Historic Trust, Inc. and the Hawthorne Cottage National Historic Site provided access to these historically significant Newfoundland and Labrador properties.

Colleagues who have shared their perspectives, critiqued our work, and brainstormed with us include Lyle Dick, a historian with Parks Canada, whose award-winning scholarship has been invaluable to us; Catherine Dempsey, former executive director of the Historic Sites Association of Newfoundland and Labrador, who introduced us to the Bartlett family and to other Newfoundland descendants of North Pole crew; and Patricia Erikson, who shared with us her insights into Josephine Peary. We also want to thank the Philadelphia Area Center for History of Science (PACHS) and Robert Peck, senior fellow at the Academy of Natural Sciences of Drexel University, for helping develop, organize, and host the *North by Degree* symposium. Phil Cronenwett and Deirdre and David Stam helped us run the conference, and film archivists Audrey Amidon (Class of 2003) and Audrey Kupferberg helped us pull together the *Explorers in Motion* film festival. We thank them and the many presenters and contributors to the conference for taking on the challenge of examining the history of Arctic exploration employing new methodologies and perspectives.

The late George Wardwell generously shared his grandfather's journals and lantern slides with us. He, along with his wife Edna, mother Phyllis, and sister Diane Wardwell James, showed us many kindnesses, sharing food and family lore with us. We also benefited from the assistance of the extended family of Robert A. Bartlett. In particular, it was an honor to meet Sam Bartlett, who regaled us with stories of some of his experiences working for his uncle, and we are grateful to Marion Bartlett, widow of Rupert Bartlett, who tolerated us repeatedly being underfoot as we searched for missing North Pole documents.

Many generations of Peary relatives in the United States and Greenland shared their insights. In particular, we thank Robert Peary Jr., Robert Peary III and his wife Inez, Edward Stafford and his wife Peggy, and Peary

Stafford in the United States, and Kale Peary, his daughter Pauline, and his grandson Hivshu in Greenland. Also, we wish to thank Peary's grandson Magssanguaq Jensen and Odaq's son Iggianguaq Odaq for helping us correctly exhibit items of Inughuit technology.

One of the joys of our positions is working with talented Bowdoin College undergraduates and interns. In addition to the Gibbons fellows mentioned above, Rebecca Genauer (Class of 2008) created archival film stations for the *Northward Over the Great Ice* exhibit, and Eli Bossin (Class of 2009) assisted with the exhibit installation. Eli, Hillary Hooke, and Alison Weisburger (Class of 2010) also presented at the *Peary's Quest for the Pole* symposium. Working as a full-time intern, Emma Bonanomi (Class of 2003) conducted research about Matthew Henson, tracked down rare Henson film footage, and presented a paper about Henson's 1909 lecture tour at both symposia. Jennifer Crane (Class of 2003), the IMLS intern, wrote and recorded an audio tour of the *Northward Over the Great Ice* exhibit, developed K–12 school outreach initiatives, and taught a week-long history camp in collaboration with the Maine Humanities Council. Hillary Hooke, a 2009–2011 museum intern, helped transcribe George Wardwell's 1905–1906 journal and maintained the North Pole historic blog. In addition, we want to thank the students enrolled in Susan A. Kaplan's "Arctic Exploration" course during fall 2009 for their insightful analyses of Arctic exploration literature and their enthusiastic contributions to the museum's North Pole centennial programs. More recently, Dana Williams (Class of 2018) and Tharunkrishna Vemulapalli (Class of 2019) conducted the Kane Lodge Foundation, Inc.–supported inventory of the Peary family's Eagle Island home.

We want to thank the employees throughout the college who have supported our endeavors, making sure bills are paid, climate-control systems operate correctly, multimedia and online presentations work, and our facilities are clean. Most particularly, we are grateful to our colleagues at the Arctic Museum who have been partners in this journey, showing dedication, high standards, creativity, and good humor. Kristi Clifford, then administrative secretary, got people, equipment, and supplies to the right places; used her search skills to track down collections; and helped organize and run events. David Maschino, exhibition designer, employed his extraordinary skills to translate our ideas into three-dimensional exhibitions and has been an invaluable sounding board for ideas. Anne Witty, then assistant curator, was deeply involved in the research, development, and execution of the Peary exhibits and programs. Her vast knowledge of things maritime and her publications helped us better understand the innovations Peary incorporated into SS *Roosevelt*. The late Nancy Wagner was a calming presence as the museum's receptionist and outreach coordinator, and Steven Bunn, exhibits technician, created finely crafted exhibit furniture. Long-term museum volunteer Mildred Jones worked tirelessly over many years to catalog thousands of photographs, helping us make sense of a vast collection and enhancing our ability to find the right photograph for any occasion.

The current Arctic Museum staff, David Maschino and Steven Bunn, as well as Michael Quigley, assistant curator; James Tanzer, receptionist and outreach coordinator; Katie Donlan, curatorial intern; KymNoelle Hopson, administrative coordinator; and Denise Linet, receptionist, assisted us in innumerable ways as we wrote this book. In addition, Michael, James, Katie, KymNoelle, and Denise helped proofread the galleys, and KymNoelle created the map.

We are grateful to Jed Lyons, president and CEO of Rowman & Littlefield, and Michael Steere, editorial director of Down East Books, for their interest in publishing a book about Peary-related people and events rarely highlighted in polar exploration literature. We appreciate Michael's editorial advice during the early stages of this endeavor and are grateful to Sarah Parke, Michael's assistant, for keeping the various parts of this project moving. We have enjoyed working with Patricia Stevenson, senior production editor at Rowman & Littlefield, who was open to our suggestions and generous with her advice as she shepherded this book through production.

INDEX

Aapilaq, 44, 119, *120*, *129*, 134
Adams, Cyrus C., 122–23
African Americans. *See* Henson, Matthew Alexander; race issues
Aleqasina, 15, 73, 112
Aleqasinnguaq, *106*
Alert, HMS, 7, 22, 93, 153
Amaunalik, *102*
American Geographical Society, 15
Amundsen, Roald, 88, 131, 147
Anderson, William R., *137*
Ane, *102*
Anniversary Lodge, 11, 12, 69
Anoritok, 33, 110, 119, *120*, 125
Aqattanguaq, 78, *104*, 112
Arctic: contemporary issues, 139–41, 143–52; darkness in, 36; geopolitical issues, 146–49
Arctic Council, 147, 149
Arctic exploration: literature on, 7; Peary's early interest in, 6–7
Arctic fox, 97, 109
Arctic hare, *34*, 97
Arctic Ocean: currents, 143–44, *145*; global warming and, 143–46
Astrup, Aivind, 11
Atangana, *14*, *102*
Avery, Tom, 139
Aviaq, *14*, *102*
Axel Heiberg Island, 28, 133

Bancroft, Ann, 137
Barker, Elsa, 134
Barnes, Jack, 35–36
Bartlett, John, 81
Bartlett, Robert A., 18, 59, 80, 81–85, *82*, *85*; and 1905–1906 expedition, 19, 21–22, 23, 28, 30–31, 82–83; and 1908–1909 expedition, 33, 34, 38, 83–84; and controversy, 127, 128
Bartlett, Sam, 81
Battle Harbour, Peary at, 44, 65, 123–24, *124*
Bennett, Floyd, 131
Bernier, Joseph E., 147
Big Lead, 25, 26, 37
Billy Bah. *See* Eqariusaq
birds, 97, *98*
Boas, Franz, 14
Bombardier, Jean-Luc, 137
Bonanomi, Emma, vi, 79, 128
Borup, George, 65, 78, 87–89, *87–88*, *104*; and 1908–1909 expedition, 33, 34, 37, 38, 61–62, 86, 87–88; and Inughuit, 105, *106*
Bowdoin College, 2–3, *4*, 63, 64, 139
Bowdoin Fjord, 11
bows and arrows, 99
Boyd, Louise, 84
bracing, 57, *58*
Bradley, John R., 117, 123
Brainard, David, 43, *87*
breaking trail, *25*, 26, 38–39, 63, 83
Bridgman, Herbert, 15, 118, 122
Brooklyn Institute, 9
Bryce, Robert, 134, 140
burros, 52
Byrd, Richard, 131, *133*

cairns, *29*, 43, *87*, 88, *88*, 153
camp stoves, 55, *56*
Canada, 146–47, 148, 151
Canadian Arctic Archipelago, 146–47
Canadian Arctic Expedition, 84

Susan A. Kaplan is a professor of anthropology and director of the Peary-MacMillan Arctic Museum and Arctic Studies Center, Bowdoin College. She received her BA from Lake Forest College and her MA and PhD from Bryn Mawr College. She is an Arctic anthropologist and archaeologist who studies prehistoric and historic Inuit responses to environmental change and contact with the West, the history of Arctic exploration, and material culture. She works primarily in northern Labrador, Canada, though projects have taken her to Alaska, Ellesmere Island, and Newfoundland as well. She was the editor of the circumpolar journal *Arctic Anthropology* for 11 years and is the author and editor of numerous research and exhibition publications. In addition to research, teaching, and overseeing museum operations, she organizes international and national symposia and develops outreach programs for the general public and northern communities. At Bowdoin she teaches courses having to do with archaeology, contemporary Arctic issues, cultures' responses to environmental changes, and human-animal relationships.

Genevieve M. LeMoine is an archaeologist and curator/registrar of the Peary-MacMillan Arctic Museum and Arctic Studies Center, Bowdoin College. She received her BA from the University of Toronto and her MA and PhD from the University of Calgary. She began working in the North as a graduate student, excavating Paleo-Eskimo sites on north Devon Island. Since then, she has worked at sites in the Mackenzie Delta, Northwest Territories; Little Cornwallis Island, Nunavut; Inglefield Land, northwestern Greenland; and northern Ellesmere Island, Nunavut (the last three as a principal investigator). Her research interests include skeletal technology, experimental archaeology, and women in prehistory. Her research has been funded by the Social Sciences and Humanities Research Council of Canada, the National Science Foundation, and the National Geographic Society. She has published the results of her research in a variety of academic journals and edited volumes and has curated exhibits on subjects ranging from climate change to Canadian Inuit art.